Margaret Mee

RETURN TO THE
AMAZON

Ruth Stiff

ROYAL
BOTANIC
GARDENS
KEW

ROYAL BOTANIC GARDENS KEW

LONDON : The Stationery Office

Designer   Richard B Jones

Published by The Stationery Office and available from:

Publications Centre
(mail, fax and telephone orders only)
PO Box 276, London SW8 5DT
Telephone orders 0171 873 9090
General enquiries 0171 873 0011
Fax orders 0171 873 8200

The Stationery Office Bookshops
49 High Holborn, London WC1V 6HB
(counter service and fax orders only)
Fax 0171 831 1326
68-69 Bull Street, Birmingham B4 6AD
0121 236 9696 Fax 0121 236 9699
33 Wine Street, Bristol BS1 2BQ
0117 9264306 Fax 0117 9294515
9-21 Princess Street, Manchester M60 8AS
0161 834 7201 Fax 0161 833 0634
16 Arthur Street, Belfast BT1 4GD
01232 238451 Fax 01232 235401
The Stationery Office Oriel Bookshop
The Friary, Cardiff CF1 4AA
01222 395548 Fax 01222 384347
71 Lothian Road, Edinburgh EH3 9AZ
(counter service only)

Customers in Scotland may
mail, telephone or fax their orders to:
Scottish Publications Sales
South Gyle Crescent, Edinburgh EH12 9EB
0131 479 3141 Fax 0131 479 3142

Accredited Agents
(see Yellow Pages)

and through good booksellers

CONTENTS

EXHIBITION SITES

Houston Museum of Natural Science
Houston
January 22 - September 21, 1997

California Academy of Sciences
San Francisco
October 18, 1997 - January 11, 1998

Dixon Gallery and Gardens
Memphis
February 7 - May 3, 1998

Huntington Library
San Marino
May 30 - August 23, 1998

Bell Museum of Natural History
University of Minnesota
Minneapolis
September 19 - December 13, 1998

Field Museum
Chicago
January 8 - April 30, 1999

National Museum of Natural History
Smithsonian Institution
Washington, D.C.
May 27 - August 20, 1999

SPONSOR'S LETTER

It is with great pleasure that we participate in this exhibition and accompanying publication. In the early days of planning, when much of what has now come to fruition was only the vaguest consideration, it was the inspiration of a close family friend, Christopher Sheridan, that caused us to recognize the full potential of this project and we thank him for his vision. The many dimensions of this program, which capture Margaret Mee's indomitable spirit, along with her passion to preserve the rain forest, her artistic genius, her courageous exploration, and her concern for the indigenous peoples of the Amazon, give this endeavor a unique quality of which we are proud to play a part.

To the many people and institutions that have worked so hard to make this undertaking a success, we congratulate you. It is truly a fitting tribute to Margaret Mee. We look forward to the continuing influence her life and work and, in some way, this exhibition will have on the preservation of one of the world's greatest natural treasures - The Amazon basin.

Cynthia and George Mitchell

PREFACE

This volume designed to accompany the exhibition 'Return to the Amazon' has mainly capitalised on the paintings and sketchbooks held at Kew, but we are most grateful to the National Museum of Natural History of the Smithsonian Institution; the Instituto de Botânica de São Paulo and a number of private individuals who by the loan of some of their collections have made this exhibition so much richer and more extensive.

The exhibition itself has only come into being through the total commitment and hard work of our North American Curator of exhibitions Ruth Stiff and her generously supportive husband Enoch. They have carried the massive burden of "making it all happen" and we most happily recognise their success in this superb exposition of Margaret Mee's work.

The conversion of Ruth Stiff's concepts for the exhibition for us all to enjoy has been through a most fruitful and close co-operation with the Houston Museum of Natural Science and more particularly the Director, Truett Latimer and his committed and dedicated staff, without which again there would be no international travelling exhibition of this calibre. Last but certainly not least, I would like to thank Cynthia and George Mitchell for their generous patronage which ensured everyone's dream came true!

Professor Sir Ghillean Prance MA, D.Phil,
DSc, FRS, FLS, FlBiol, FRGS

ACKNOWLEDGEMENTS

Margaret Mee: Return to the Amazon is an exhibition program that has resulted from the joint efforts of many individuals and institutions both in this country and abroad. It is a pleasure to be able to express my warmest thanks to those who have contributed so generously to the success of this project.

The initial concept for this exhibition originated several years ago with Professor Grenville Lucas of Kew, who was then Keeper of the Herbarium and Library. Kew's first international exhibition, "Flowers from the Royal Gardens of Kew," a project on which Gren and I had worked closely, was just ending its successful two and one-half year tour of the United States, and plans were being formulated for future travelling exhibitions. Since its inception, Gren has kept a supportive eye on the project, and I am greatly indebted to him for his wise counsel, invaluable help and unstinting support. I am also grateful to both him and his wife, Shirley, for their gracious hospitality, demonstrated on countless occasions, by allowing me to stay in their historic home, situated within the wall of Kew Gardens.

My colleagues at the Royal Botanic Gardens, Kew extended themselves to an extraordinary degree to ensure the success of the project. I am grateful to the Director, Professor Sir Ghillean Prance, not only for enriching this catalogue with his essay but also for generously lending a number of artefacts from his private collection to the exhibition. I am particularly indebted to Dr Simon Mayo, who provided invaluable assistance with the catalogue and graciously allowed me to benefit from his research. Special thanks to Mr David Field for his useful advice on the selection of Spruce artefacts for the exhibition. Dr Philip Cribb and Ms Sarah Thomas, along with my American colleagues Ms Bobbi Angell and Mrs Pauline Cartledge, were most helpful in assisting with the botanical notes for the catalogue. Mr Ray Desmond, Mrs Cheryl Piggott and Dr Brinsley Burbidge gave me much encouragement and practical help, and my particular thanks to Ray for his very helpful comments on my manuscript. My special thanks also go to Andrew McRobb for the excellent photography produced for this catalogue and to Ann Lucas for her assistance with administrative issues. Miss Sylvia FitzGerald and the staff of Kew Library were very resourceful in facilitating my search for information. I owe a special debt of gratitude to Miss Marilyn Ward and Miss Kate Edmondson who worked closely with me in selecting and assembling the works of art, and preparing the exhibition for travel. Without their diligent and expert assistance this project could not have been realised.

A wide variety of talents and expertise is essential for a project such as this one. The staff of the Houston Museum of Natural Science, coorganizer of this exhibition, ably and enthusiastically played many roles deserving of heartfelt thanks. I am indebted to Dr Truett Latimer, Director of the Houston Museum of Natural Science, for his leadership in this collaborative effort. Appreciative thanks are due to Mr Bruce Behnfeldt, for designing the exhibition, with the help of his skilled and imaginative colleagues; to Mr Hayden Valdes, for his thoughtful guidance; and to

Dr Nancy Greig, for the invaluable scientific contribution that she provided. I would also like to acknowledge the many courtesies extended by Ms Lisa Rebori, Ms Dina Kohleffel and Ms Linda Haston as well as other members of the staff, and to thank them for their pragmatic assistance in the areas of collections management, financial development and administrative direction.

The extended Houston community played an essential role in ensuring the success of this exhibition. I should like to express my special thanks to Cynthia and George Mitchell, whose generous patronage has made this exhibition possible. Cynthia's commitment to this endeavour has been a vital source of inspiration and I am particularly grateful for her warm encouragement and friendship. Ms Dancie Ware and Ms Ellen Wagnon of Dancie Perugini Ware Public Relations have been critical in the fund raising and public relations efforts.

The Garden Club of America, whose leadership and members have embraced this project, has provided invaluable support on a national and regional level. Special thanks are due to Mrs Zinkie Benton of the River Oaks Garden Club and to Mrs Renvia Lander of the Garden Club of Houston for their gracious assistance with activities associated with the exhibition. Other individuals in numerous cities who have been especially helpful include Mrs Bonnie Martin, Mrs Mary Ott, Mrs Jean Carton, Mrs Hattie Purtell, Mrs Lil Bruce, Mrs Elvira Butz, Ms Polly Penney, and Mrs Colles Larkin.

I extend my sincere thanks to the following members of the Margaret Mee Amazon Trust: Sir Michael Newington, the Hon. Christopher McLaren and his wife Jane, Professor Richard Schultes, Dr Raymond Harley, Dr Shirley Sherwood, Mrs Marion Morrison, Mr Martin Pendred, Mr Michael Daly and his wife Juliet, and Mrs Elizabeth Edmunds. For sharing his expertise, I am especially grateful to Mr Tony Morrison, whose research laid the ground for subsequent scholarship. My own research was greatly facilitated by his efforts. Special thanks to Dr John Hemming for his historical advice which helped shape the exhibition in its formative stages and to Margaret Mee's family, Mr Greville Mee and his wife Elisabeth, who have been unstinting in their enthusiasm and kind support.

The Brazilian Ambassador to the United States, Paulo Tarso Flecha de Lima, has shown a keen interest in this project since its inception and his encouragement has been greatly appreciated. In addition, the cooperation and generosity of the Brazilian Fundação Botânica Margaret Mee, the sister organization of the Margaret Mee Amazon Trust, has been essential to the success of the project. In particular, I should like to thank Mr Philip Jenkins, Chairman, and his wife Molly for their unwavering commitment to this endeavour, and to Mr William Searight for his personal and professional help as well as the warm hospitality he and his wife so graciously provided during my travels to Brazil. I am also indebted to Mrs Sylvia de Botton Brautigam, Ms Sue Loram, Professor Luiz Emydio de Mello Filho, the late Roberto Burle Marx and the late Professor Aristides Azevedo Pacheco Leão for their many kindnesses.

Special thanks is due to Mr Lewis Reid of The American Society for the Royal Botanic Gardens, Kew, headquartered in San Francisco, and his skilled assistant, Ms Brenda Mahoney, for their administrative and logistical support concerning the financial aspect of this project. I also benefited from the thoughtful suggestions of Mrs Mary Reid, and greatly appreciated her lovely meals and gracious hospitality during my stays with the Reids at Hog Hill.

I would like to express my gratitude to Mr Gregory Long, Director, Dr Brian Boom, Vice President for Science, and the staff of the New York Botanical Garden for their essential research support. I am particularly indebted to Mr John Reed and Mrs Judy Reed for the vital assistance that they, along with Don Wheeler, provided at the Library, and for their kind hospitality. Dr Scott Mori and Ms Carol Gracie were an invaluable resource to me on a research visit to the Rio Negro, and I am further indebted to Carol for her superb photographic efforts, continued research during subsequent journeys to Amazonia, and also for her introduction to Mr Moacir Fortes of Manaus, whose logistical assistance made possible the procurement of an Amazonian canoe for the exhibition. Special thanks to Ms. Anne Hall for her assistance with translation during my travels in eastern Brazil.

The Milwaukee Public Museum deserves special mention for its important contribution during the early development of this project. In particular, I should like to thank Dr Martin Dibben, Mr Jim Kelly, Ms Connie Brand Sayas, and Ms Carol Ann Piggens for their shared expertise which helped shape the exhibition in its most formative stage.

A special word of appreciation is due to the directors and staff of the participatory museums for cooperating in every way to make the exhibition a success. In particular I would like to thank Dr Willard Boyd, Dr Peter Crane, Ms Laura Gates, and Dr Willard White of the Field Museum; Dr Evelyn Handler, Ms Daphne Derven, Ms Judy Procopek, Ms Laurel Sabino, and Ms Mimi Schreiber of the California Academy of Sciences; Dr Edward Nygren and Dr Amy Myers of the Huntington Library and Art Collections; Mr Joseph Czestochowski of the Dixon Gallery and Gardens; Mr Scott Lanyon of the Bell Museum; and Dr Thomas Lovejoy, Mr Robert Fri, Dr Warren Wagner, Ms Marjorie Stoller, Mr Lawrence O'Reilly and Ms Alice Tangerini of the Smithsonian Institution; and Dr Adauto Ivo Milanez, Ms Carmen Sylvia Zocchio Fidalgo, and Mrs Beulah Coe Teixeira of the São Paulo Botanical Institute.

The exhibition has been enhanced by loans from both public institutions and private collectors. We are greatly indebted to the National Museum of Natural History, Smithsonian Institution, and the São Paulo Botanical Institute for their willingness to lend artworks from their collections and to Mr and Mrs Greville Mee and also Mr and Mrs Walter Schwab for their generosity in sharing their works of art with us.

I gratefully acknowledge the assistance of numerous individuals who have given so selflessly of their time on behalf of this project. In particular I would like to thank Pia and Simon Pearce, Mary and Bob Feind, and Karen and Joe Branch for their interest and caring support and for their many kindnesses to my children. My dedicated assistant, Nicola Prahl, helped in myriad ways at all hours, often at a moment's notice, and special thanks must go to Joan Shank, for her tireless assistance with administrative matters.

I am immensely grateful to my family, Bernard and Eugenia Stiff, for their enthusiastic support and kind ways. My sister, Ellen Therrien, greatly assisted with my research and was a constant encouragement with her kindred passion for flowers. For the understanding, enduring patience, and flexibility of my sons, Andrew, Christian and Tyler, I shall always be grateful. My deep appreciation and gratitude goes to my husband, Enoch, who shared my enthusiasm for the project and demonstrated his unfailing support with inexhaustible kindness.

Ruth L. A. Stiff, MALS FLS
Curator, North American Exhibitions, RBG, Kew

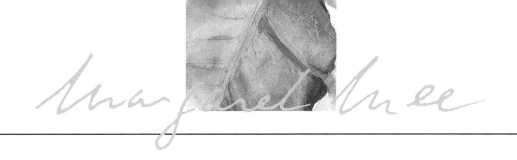

INTRODUCTION

For more than a century, the Royal Botanic Gardens, Kew has recorded in water colour the blooms, fruits and appropriate foliage of new or rare plants that flower in the Gardens. This vast and diverse collection of botanical drawings, preserved in the Kew library, is essential to botanical science, capturing all the essential characteristics of the plants which prove so transitory in life. They also represent the extraordinarily high quality work of premier botanical artists, with their botanical accuracy and detailed analytical studies, the essential tool for taxonomists. As works of art, they express the ephemeral beauty of the subject matter as well as the aesthetic skills of the artists with their differing styles.

On occasion, other outstanding collections of paintings have been given to Kew, allowing them to be available, in perpetuity, for research and, when appropriate for exhibition purposes. In such a manner, this special collection of Margaret Mee paintings, purchased by the Margaret Mee Amazon Trust, was presented to Kew. This, however, was no ordinary gift, as it was a realization of Margaret Mee's dream, a vision eloquently described by Simon Mayo in his essay for this publication. As part of that dream Margaret, shortly before her death, helped to establish the Margaret Mee Amazon Trust which undertook the task of purchasing the large number of Margaret's paintings, field sketchbooks and notebooks which today reside at Kew.

The collection, however, was only one part of the fulfilment of Margaret's dream. Its other element was to provide resources for Brazilian artists and botanists to study and learn at Kew and other major botanical institutions in the United Kingdom and the United States. The responsibilities of the Trust have now been passed to the Kew Foundation and Friends as the Trust has been wound up having completed its primary mission. However, to ensure a long and continuing programme for scholars able to benefit for the concept, the Foundation and Friends at Kew will carry on raising money for scholars coming to Britain, with the Friends of Kew in the United States seeking funding for Brazilians to study in appropriate botanical institutes in America. In Brazil, Fundação Botânica Margaret Mee will continue to seek local support whilst also selecting potential candidates for scholarships.

Margaret, I am sure, would be very happy to see how her works of art continue to inspire and lead. I have no doubt that these paintings, whether seen in this volume or perhaps more excitingly in the exhibition, will help you to understand why this outstanding lady has inspired so many scientists, conservationists and artists to take up the cause of protecting our fragile planet and its life-supporting flora.

Professor G Ll Lucas OBE BSc FLS FRGS

The Royal Botanic Gardens, Kew - A Brief History

Ray Desmond

One wonders how many people who visit the Royal Botanic Gardens at Kew for relaxation and to admire its floral displays are aware of the institution's other activities. Do they know it has a fascinating history extending back over two and a half centuries? In 1718, the Prince and Princess of Wales (the future King George II and Queen Caroline) acquired a house and its grounds in Richmond, Surrey, attracted by its rural setting on the banks of the River Thames. That royal property was the genesis of the Royal Botanic Gardens.

Queen Caroline, who had developed an interest in gardens in her native Germany, resolved to create a fashionable garden at Richmond Lodge, the name of the property she and her husband intended to make a summer residence. Charles Bridgeman, later appointed Royal Gardener, whom she commissioned to landscape the gardens, was a key figure in a trend at the beginning of the eighteenth century to rid English gardens of their formal elements (vistas and avenues, canals and fountains, parterres and topiary), turning instead to Nature for inspiration. His transformation of Caroline's estate still retained traces of formality, but he introduced what a contemporary writer described as "pleasing irregularity", that is, paths meandering through sprawling woodland overlooking cultivated fields and pheasant grounds. These innovations which imitated the countryside were generally applauded, but what drew the crowds to Richmond Lodge were some of the garden buildings designed by William Kent, then at the beginning of his career. His temples, pavilion and dairy were in the classical idiom, conventional and rather bland, but he showed originality in two extraordinary edifices, the Hermitage and Merlin's Cave. The former housed busts of distinguished British scientists and philosophers in tasteful rooms behind a facade of roughhewn stone. Merlin's Cave, capped by a cluster of thatched conical roofs, displayed an astonishing tableau of six life-size wax figures representing the magician Merlin and Queen Elizabeth with attendants of uncertain identity. Stephen Duck, a minor poet, was custodian of this bizarre concept. It became the talk of London; several enterprising inns attracted customers by presenting their own version of Merlin's Cave. George II dismissed it as "childish, silly stuff".

Frederick Prince of Wales, his eldest son, leased an old timber-framed house on an adjacent estate in Kew in 1731. One wonders why he chose to live so close to his parents with whom he was on very bad terms. An act of defiance or reconciliation, perhaps? Queen Caroline is on record as having described Frederick as "the greatest ass, and the greatest liar . . . and the greatest beast in the whole world and . . . I most heartily wish he was out of it". Whatever his failings, Frederick was undoubtedly a man of taste: he collected paintings, played the cello, and towards the end of his short life, gardened enthusiastically at Kew. He gradually enlarged his small garden by purchasing or leasing neighboring fields where he planted many trees and began forming a lake. He had planned to erect an assortment of garden buildings in the cultural style of other nations, but only the chinoiserie House of Confucius was built before his death in 1751. His widow,

The Palm House, designed by Decimus Burton, was completed in 1848
under the directorship of Sir William Jackson Hooker

Augusta Dowager Princess of Wales, devoted much of her wealth to achieving her late husband's vision of an exotic Kew.

She relied upon the horticultural expertise of her friend, Lord Bute, in improving her estate of 110 acres. Bute may have been instrumental in introducing her to William Chambers, a young architect whom she engaged to teach architecture to the Prince of Wales (the future King George III) and also to design garden buildings. Only a few of them have survived to the present day: some temples, an elegant Orangery, a Ruined Arch conceived as a Roman relic, and the ten-storey Pagoda, probably Kew's best known feature. Most had been built cheaply and quickly, never intended to last for long. Chambers carefully positioned them in the landscaped garden against shrubbery or facing the broad lake or raised prominently on mounds. Georgian Kew became a place of pilgrimage for discerning tourists.

They were also drawn by a notable collection of trees and flowers concentrated mainly in a small botanic garden of some nine acres. Here novelty or rarity, rather than decorative appeal, was the criterion for selecting plants. This botanic garden was perhaps the most significant development since it anticipated Kew's future role.

When Augusta's eldest son ascended the throne as George III in 1760, he inherited Richmond Lodge. 'Capability' Brown, who he employed to relandscape Queen Caroline's garden, destroyed with typical ruthlessness Charles Bridgeman's layout and William Kent's buildings, including the notorious Merlin's Cave. He substituted clumps of trees on undulating lawns sloping to the river. When George III inherited his mother's Kew dwelling on her death in 1772, he made it a summer residence and housed some of his children in Kew Palace nearby. The thatched Queen's Cottage, still to be seen at Kew, was a favorite haunt near the menagerie, a place for picnics for the royal family. In 1802, the King merged the two royal gardens into one estate.

Joseph Banks was presented to George III in 1771 when *H.M.S. Endeavour,* under the command of Captain James Cook, returned from a scientific expedition to the Pacific. Banks, a wealthy Lincolnshire landowner, had paid his own passage and that of his eight companions in order to study the wildlife and vegetation collected during the voyage. An amateur naturalist with a preference for botany, Banks soon found himself advising the King on the management of the royal gardens at Kew. Francis Masson, a gardener there, dispatched to South Africa in 1772, was the first of a succession of plant collectors Banks sent abroad. He used his friendship with the King and his presidency of the Royal Society to persuade diplomats, military personnel and traders to collect plants for Kew whenever they were overseas. Through its wealth of flowers, he was determined to make Kew Europe's premier garden.

Plant collectors in Banks's day frequently operated in little-explored territory, with poor communications, and among suspicious or even hostile inhabitants. Tropical diseases were an occupational hazard. Unfortunately, many of the plants they collected at great risk to themselves never survived the long sea voyages to Europe. So, it was always an occasion for celebration when Kew's gardeners restored some ailing plant to health, coaxing it into flower. By 1813, about 11,000 species, many from abroad and new to science, were in cultivation. A staunch imperialist, Banks aimed to make Kew "a great botanical house for the empire". He changed a royal retreat into a botanic garden, with links with newly emerging botanic gardens in the British colonies. Kew, which Banks once affectionately described as his "favourite establishment", had at last achieved international recognition.

The death of both the King and Banks in 1820 robbed Kew of royal patronage and firm leadership. King George IV showed little interest in the establishment, choosing to use the services of W.T. Aiton, its head gardener, to supervise the planting of the royal gardens at Windsor and the Brighton Pavilion. This neglect of Kew led to an alarming decline when the Lord Steward's department, which funded it, began cutting back on expenditure. Few plant collectors were now employed, glasshouses were overcrowded and in a bad state of repair, lawns had degenerated into scrub, and agricultural crops were grown near the Pagoda.

In 1837, the year of Queen Victoria's coronation, the *Gardener's Gazette* complained that "the state of the place is slovenly and discreditable and that of the plants disgracefully dirty". The accession of Queen Victoria and the consequent loss of revenue from Hanover gave the Treasury an excuse to review the funding of the Royal Household. The royal gardens presented an obvious target for economies. A working party, headed by the eminent botanist, John Lindley, was instructed to investigate them and in particular to make specific proposals on the future status of Kew Gardens. Lindley's report in 1838 urged the State to assume responsibility for Kew, making it "worthy of the country", transforming it into "a powerful means of promoting national science". In other words, Lindley was advocating the creation of a National Botanic Garden. This was not the sort of advice the Treasury had expected. It did what is so often done with undesirable reports - shelved it. However, when lively protests from scientists and questions by members of Parliament followed a clandestine attempt to dismember Kew, the Government capitulated. In June, 1840, it announced that Kew would cease to be a private royal garden and would be transferred to the Office of Woods and Forests. The Professor of Botany at the University of Glasgow, Sir William Jackson Hooker, was appointed its first Director.

Hooker, who had desperately wanted to be an active part of the scientific scene in London, had for some years made it be known that he would welcome the chance of succeeding Aiton at Kew. Apart from John Lindley, he was perhaps the most eligible candidate. Not only was he an eminent botanist and a prolific author and editor, but he had also managed a small botanic garden in Glasgow. His duties were confined to Kew's nine-acre botanic garden, while the Pleasure Grounds which constituted the major part of the estate remained under Aiton's control.

In the absence of any directives from the Office of Woods and Forests, Hooker made the enlargement of the botanic garden and the construction of more glasshouses his first priorities. Within a very short time, he had negotiated the transfer of over 40 acres from the Pleasure Grounds, and when Aiton, now approaching 80, eventually retired in 1845 the rest of the estate passed to Hooker. Now he had adequate space for more glasshouses. The architect, Decimus Burton, with assistance from the constructional engineer, Richard Turner, designed a curvilinear Palm House over 360 feet long and 100 feet wide. Next to the Pagoda, it is the most eye-catching feature at Kew today, a tribute to Victorian engineering skills.

It served as a convenient focal point for William Nesfield's relandscaping of the grounds. A grand processional way (the Broad Walk) approached it from the Main Gates on Kew Green, and three vistas radiated from its west side into a new Arboretum which absorbed much of the old Pleasure Grounds. A lake reduced the density of trees, and a miniature valley formed in the eighteenth century by 'Capability' Brown, offered sanctuary to a collection of newly introduced Himalayan rhododendrons. Some space was spared in the Arboretum for a sensational new acquisition, the giant South American water lily, Victoria amazonia. All these improvements, which greatly expanded the quantity and variety of trees and flowers on display, made Kew one of London's most popular resorts.

One of Hooker's annual reports defined "health, pleasure and instruction" as being among Kew's objectives. A museum, quickly adapted from an old fruit store in 1848, provided "instruction". It was devoted to economic botany - the first of its kind in Britain - housing specimens of fibers, textiles, drugs, dyes, vegetable oils, timbers and artifacts gathered from all over the world. Prominence was given to the produce of British colonies. A purpose-built museum was erected in 1857 to accommodate a deluge of donations from individuals and international exhibitions. Even Sir William Chambers's Orangery was converted into a timber museum.

Hooker, however, never lost sight of the fact that Kew was more than a place of relaxation and popular instruction. A botanic garden should offer facilities to study the world's vegetation. Since only a fraction of it could ever be grown, it needed the resources of an herbarium or repository of dried specimens, systematically arranged and labeled. Hooker generously allowed visiting botanists access to his own herbarium, then one of the largest in private hands. This and several other collections bequeathed to Kew in Hooker's lifetime formed the nucleus of an official herbarium.

While he was reforming Kew, Hooker never adopted an exclusively parochial attitude. He aspired to restoring Kew's international status. He saw it exercising a paternal interest in the botanic gardens in the British Empire, offering them advice, finding personnel to run them, even supplying them with stock. "It has, indeed, been our especial object to cultivate what may be useful and valuable for our colonies", he wrote in his 1850 annual report. Under him, Kew functioned as an entrepôt in a global traffic in plants and seeds, obtaining specimens from one country for cultivation in another, the aim always being the diversification of colonial agricultural and horticultural resources. The successful transfer of Cinchona, the source of quinine, from South America to India during the 1860s, was in Hooker's own words, "one of the most important horticultural operations in which as Director of this establishment, it has been my privilege to cooperate".

Obviously, the plant resources of the Empire could not be efficiently developed without first identifying them. Hooker proposed botanical surveys in a series of colonial floras descriptively listing the plants of a country or region. Before he died in 1865, he had initiated the publication of floras of the British West Indies, Hong Kong, Australia and South Africa. Sir William Hooker left to his son, who followed him as Director, a garden that had clearly defined objectives, that enjoyed the support of botanists and gardeners, the affection of the British public, and universal respect.

Joseph Dalton Hooker, like his father before him, had disputes with those government ministers who insisted on lavish floral displays more appropriate to a public park than to a botanic garden. A bitter confrontation with one particular minister involved Parliament, the intervention of the Prime Minister, and seriously threatened the survival of Kew as a scientific institution. As a distinguished taxonomist and phytogeographer whose independent researches assisted his friend Charles Darwin, Joseph Hooker resolutely defended the integrity of Kew as a botanic garden. He was responsible for adding the first wing to the Herbarium in 1877. The Jodrell Laboratory, opened in the same year, offered facilities for studying the structure and physiology of plants, then a new area of research for Kew. He launched the publication of the Index Kewensis with financial backing from the Darwin family. The first four volumes of this record of the botanical names of seed-bearing plants appeared between 1892 and 1895, and has been kept up-to-date with regular supplements. Now available on compact disc, it is an indispensable tool for all plant taxonomists.

This emphasis on science in no way diminished Kew's involvement in imperial affairs. Much of this was delegated to William Thiselton-Dyer, the Assistant Director. In 1876, he took charge of a huge consignment of rubber seeds from South America. The occasion has since been frequently denounced as a reprehensible act of 'smuggling' them out of an unsuspecting Brazil, but new evidence has cast doubt on this charge. Within a matter of a few months, Kew had raised 1,900 seedlings which were dispatched to a new government plantation in Ceylon, the beginning of the island's rubber trade. The Malayan rubber plantations were also established with stock from Kew. Once a new crop had been successfully grown in any colony, it was Kew's policy to withdraw from the project, leaving its progress to commerce and local botanic gardens. As many of these botanic gardens were manned by Kew-trained gardeners or nominees, good working relations with Kew were assured. No one ever doubted Joseph Hooker's assertion that Kew was "the botanical headquarters of the British Empire and its dependencies".

Evocative scenes of colonial landscape, its forests and flowers were painted on the spot by that indefatigable traveler, Marianne North. She and Margaret Mee had much in common: both loved flowers passionately, both painted obsessively, and both were indifferent to personal discomfort. In 1882, Miss North presented Kew with over 800 of her oil paintings and a gallery in which to house them. She personally supervised their installation in a tight mosaic of pictures that completely covered the walls: the result is an extraordinary, if not unique, presentation. It is worth a visit to Kew just to see her gallery.

Marianne North's depictions, although reasonably accurate, lack the precision of the work of a botanical artist such as Margaret Mee, who incorporated in her flower portraits all their distinguishing features so that their identification is indisputable. A flower painter, on the other hand, not constrained by such requirements, is more often concerned with conveying the general character or the personality of a plant. Francis Bauer, an Austrian botanical artist, was employed by Sir Joseph Banks at Kew from 1790. For the next 50 years, he meticulously recorded in vibrant watercolors some of the new and exotic plants blooming in the royal garden. William Hood Fitch was trained in the discipline of botanical art by Sir William Hooker. His bravura style captured the monumentality of the *Victoria amazonica* and the dazzle of orchids. The camera has not yet superseded the interpretative skills of botanical artists who are still employed at Kew and other botanic gardens.

Sir Joseph Hooker left Kew in 1885 to enjoy a long and productive retirement. (The reason why so many botanists, especially taxonomists, live to an advanced old age may be that they seldom stop working!). His son-in-law, Thiselton-Dyer, defended just as firmly Kew's identity as a botanic garden, and involved it even more closely with schemes to advance colonial horticulture. He was an unrepentant imperialist who, largely through the issues of the *Kew Bulletin*, which he started in 1887, established Kew as a center of economic intelligence for government departments and commerce. The Colonial Office, the Foreign Office and the India Office called upon it for advice. It could be a matter of new or improved vegetable fibers, or the eradication of plant diseases, or the recruitment of staff for horticultural duties overseas. Kew participated in a scheme to set up small botanic stations primarily for the experimental cultivation of new crops; the first were installed in the West Indies during the 1880s, followed by others in Africa and other colonial territories. When an Imperial Department of Agriculture for the West Indies was created in 1898, it was Kew's Assistant Director who took charge of it. Its success led to the formation of similar departments in India, Africa and Malaya. Joseph Chamberlain, then Secretary of State for the Colonies, acknowledged his department's indebtedness to Kew in Parliament in 1898:

"I do not think it is too much to say that at the present time there are several of our important Colonies which own whatever prosperity they possess to the knowledge and experience of, and the assistance given by, the authorities at Kew Gardens".

When Thiselton-Dyer was not advising the Colonial Office, he was busy improving Kew's landscape. He was not the first Director convinced he had a talent as a garden designer. Sir Joseph Hooker had laid out vistas and avenues, enlarged his father's lake, and formed a pinetum. Thiselton-Dyer designed a large rock garden supposed to resemble a Pyrenean watercourse, planted thousands of bulbs in the ground in a naturalistic manner, and transformed the mound bearing the Temple of Eolus into a wild garden. He eventually succeeded in abolishing elaborate summer bedding schemes, long considered to be out of character in a botanic garden.

He was the last of the Hooker dynasty at Kew. When he passed the reins of office to David Prain in 1905, he approved the appointment of a man with 20 years service in India, for the most part at the Calcutta Botanic Garden. In 1911, Prain arranged for the erection of a full-scale facsimile of a sixteenth century Japanese gateway near the Pagoda. It has just been restored by Japanese craftsmen whose replication of intricate carved wood panels confirm that they have not lost any of their traditional skills. The placid tenor of Prain's administration was disrupted in 1913 by suffragettes who destroyed plants in the orchid houses and burned down the restaurant. His successor, Arthur Hill, enjoyed a sort of ambassadorial role, touring the British dominions, the last spokesman for Imperial Kew.

The 1939-45 war and the years of post-war austerity had imposed severe financial constraints on Kew. It needed the energy and initiative of George Taylor, appointed Director in 1956, to revitalize the institution. The ground received cosmetic treatment in time for the bicentenary celebrations in 1959. Ten years later, Her Majesty The Queen opened a new period garden behind Kew Palace. The Queen's Garden, as it is now called, displays features contemporary with seventeenth century Kew Palace: a formal parterre, clipped box, a mound, a pleached hornbeam walk, a sunken garden, a gazebo and statues. The plants grown there are those that would have been found in English gardens of the 1630s.

When the old Jodrell Laboratory was completely rebuilt in 1965, cytogenetics was included in its research program. A fourth wing was added to the Herbarium in 1969. Little space now remained at Kew for any further development. Fortunately another garden was found in 1965 at Wakehurst Place in Sussex, an estate owned by the National Trust. It has provided some 500 acres of fertile soil, a high rainfall, and no industrial pollution. Its outstanding array of trees, planted in the early decades of this century (many were lost during the violent storm in 1987), have been joined by Kew's major collections of *Rhododendron, Acer, Nothofagus and Betula* and other genera likely to thrive on a more hospitable site. Apart from a walled garden near the Tudor mansion, the planting is informal on an undulating landscape, with a broad lake and spectacular outcrops of massive sandstone boulders.

As well as reversing Kew's stagnation, Sir George Taylor prepared the way for further improvements by his successors. The Palm House and the Temperate House, both Grade I listed buildings, have been extensively restored. The old boiler house beneath the Palm House now exhibits living plants of marine habitats - rocky shore and salt marsh, mangrove swamp and coral reef. A cluster of 26 glasshouses was demolished to provide a site for the Princess of Wales Conservatory. Opened in 1987, this glasshouse, the largest in the world, is equipped with an automated system which controls ten climatic zones and several micro-areas, ranging from the dry desert to the moist tropics. In 1994, Her Majesty The Queen opened an extension to the Jodrell Laboratory to accommodate laboratories for molecular systematics, biochemistry and biological interactions. The Australian House was adapted in 1995 to present a dramatic interpretation of the story of plant evolution. All these are notable achievements, but perhaps the most significant event occurred in 1984 when responsibility for Kew Gardens was vested in a Board of Trustees. The Director, currently Professor Sir Ghillean Prance, advises the Trustees.

Kew has come a long way since its formative years as a royal garden. It now cultivates about ten per cent of the world's species of seed plants and ferns. More than 4,000 species are stored in the Seed Bank. The Herbarium with 6,700,000 specimens can claim to be the world's largest. There are some 80,000 plant products in the economic plant collections. The Library's fine collection of herbals, color plate books and standard texts is complemented by the works of many outstanding botanical artists and flower painters. New material is constantly being added to its 175,000 drawings and prints. Among recent accessions are Margaret Mee's superb paintings, the subject of this exhibition.

In 1990, the Friends of Kew was launched to inform the public of Kew's collections and activities through an attractive magazine, lectures and social gatherings. They help in fundraising events and provide a corps of trained guides to escort parties of visitors. The Friends make a valuable contribution to Kew's mission, which is "to enable better management of the earth's environment by increasing knowledge and understanding of the plant kingdom".

Margaret Mee – Life and Legacy

Dr Simon Mayo

In the last few days of 1976 I found myself, a greenhorn botanist, in the tropics for the first time. We had landed at Rio en route to Bahia and our expedition leader Ray Harley, an old friend of Margaret and Greville Mee, called them from the airport in the hope of an early morning cup of tea. Soon we were winding our way up into Santa Teresa, the old suburb which cascades down steep slopes towards the city centre, and eventually we arrived in Rua Julio Otoni at the Mee's distinctive house, perched on a precipitous slope in the midst of large jackfruit trees. The sensations of those first few hours in Brazil are engraved in my memory, and forever associated with Margaret and Greville's garden and street: there was a deafening siren of morning cicadas, brilliant sun on white walls, the weight of the heat and humidity, intense greenness and a rich profusion of vegetation out of which sprang scarlet and purple bromeliad spikes; hanging orchids, aroids and the delicate foliage of ferns crowded around us. Plants seemed to sprout from every possible point, regardless of form and decorum, a veritable mirror to the spirit of the city: dramatic, exotic, graceful and seductive, cruelly careless of life, perfect poised beauty suddenly encountered, anciently wise and anciently dangerous.

In the midst of this riot, Margaret's gentle stooping figure greeted us, fussing over Greville and the dangers of the street. Still mesmerized, I found myself drinking tea from elegant Wedgwood china on the terrace, while Margaret tended to her hummingbirds and their sugar water, and called Ray over to show him her latest plants. The conversation ebbed and flowed and the names of the famous and adventurous were thick in the air - Richard Evans Schultes, Ghillean Prance, João Murça Pires, William Rodrigues, Walter Egler, Adolfo Ducke, Richard Spruce, Robin Hanbury-Tenison, and many others. Margaret had very clear large blue eyes that were totally beguiling. She seemed, as everyone says, fragile; I thought her rather elderly and frail - but suddenly she would erupt into a giggle about some story or event, and her youthful spirit shone forth.

Within an hour or two, eminent persons began to gather. In the space of a single day I met Dr Aristides Leão - the President of Brazil's Academy of Sciences, Dr Guido Pabst the orchid specialist, Dr Graziela Barroso - Brazil's most eminent botanist, and Roberto Burle Marx - the world famous landscape artist. This all took place as though previously planned, but it had in fact been improvised with the casual, easy etiquette that is characteristic of Rio. The talk was of the Amazon, the forest, the destruction, the discovery of new plants and their secrets. Margaret had an inexhaustible enthusiasm for plants and the forest - whether the plant was new or old was less important than her tremendous gift for conveying the pure excitement of the discovery of a new flower, a corolla unfolding, a shape rendered in its perfect sculpture, its pristine ineffable newness. Her discovery was your discovery. She was, apparently, entirely free of that tendency so common in naturalists to hunt, to trap, to keep and hoard. Power and knowledge. Margaret discovered rather than hunted, and communicated her discovery like a vision made with new eyes. Her power was to reveal. Her great friend and mentor, Roberto Burle Marx, expressed this perfectly:

© Tony Morrison

Margaret Mee, aged seventy-nine,
on her fifteenth journey to
Amazonia in May 1988

"...to seek out a plant, bring it from its obscurity and reveal it to those who are inspired by Nature, is a true discovery..."

The house was full of travel and botanical books, mostly concerned with Brazilian flora and the Amazon. The atmosphere seemed almost old-world. Classical music floated up from the sitting room on the lower storey, where Greville played his immense collection of LPs. It seemed a paradise of elegant repose, until, opening the front gate, the visitor was whisked into the turbulent, electric current of Rio's street life - with its sensation of heart-stopping excitement or danger at every corner. This, as I grew to understand in later visits, was for Margaret a place of rest in the intervals between her extraordinary painting expeditions to the Amazon.

It has taken time for me to appreciate just how special were Margaret Mee and her plant paintings. Others, after all, have journeyed in the Amazon and had adventures, and yet others have painted beautiful plant portraits. Margaret, however, was a great deal more than merely an Amazon traveller who painted plants. First impressions could be deceptive. Her home, so peaceful and cultured in contrast to the rigours of the frontier life on which she thrived. Her fear of Rio's streets, when her own indomitable courage shone so bright and strong. Her bird-like physique, which endured and overcame hardships that would have floored many a muscle-bound wannabe. Her paintings of beautiful plants, seemingly denizens of uncharted and eternal forests without limit - but in reality visions of a vanishing era, of plants and forests disappearing one by one into oblivion in the relentless war that our human species wages on the world. It is this sensation that Margaret was engaged head-on in a tremendous struggle that gives her work and life zest and adventure and makes her such a strong inspiration. She had enormous charisma, a finely wrought and courageous spirit, a special poise and energy, even in repose, and a quick and whole-hearted compassion. She was loved by many who knew her, particularly in Brazil, with whose deeply spiritual people Margaret's own "gênio" kindled instant and profound empathy. That this power could move millions was shown in the last weeks of her life when she captured the hearts and minds of American audiences in her tremendously successful appearances on the McNeill-Lehrer show, and more recently, in 1994, the Beija Flor Samba School of her home city of Rio featured her life in their stunning Carnaval display that was seen by at least 150 million people - an extraordinary tribute to her success in reaching out to ordinary folk.

In the introduction to her diaries ("Margaret Mee - In Search of Flowers of the Amazon Forests", Nonesuch Expeditions, 1988), Tony Morrison has given us the best published account of Margaret's life, from her birth in 1909 near Chesham in southern England, to shortly before her death in a car accident in Leicester on 30th November 1988. Here it is clear that her character was forged in other, earlier tests. Many of the qualities that underpin her Amazon endeavours had already been evident in her twenties when she threw herself into the politics and dangers of left wing opposition to fascism in the inter-war period. As a young trade unionist she made an impressive showing as a public speaker, committed to strong ideals with the fortitude to endure the hardships along the way. Her risky travels to Berlin and France in the thirties also testify to a devil-may-care adventurousness. Margaret was no solemn, humourless zealot, but a free spirit. Morrison's account suggests that the stories of her globe-trotting grandfather John Henry Churchman may have started her along this road.

She showed her artistic talent early, fostered by her Aunt Nell, a children's book illustrator; later she went to Art School in Watford, north of London. It seems inescapable, as Tony Morrison's biography suggests, that her childhood and adolescence in the green fields and wolds of England should have left their mark in her love for nature. But politics, fascism and the war intervened, pushing aside other considerations and it wasn't until peace came in 1945 that she picked up the trail of her vocation, attending the St Martin's School of Art and, in 1947, the Camberwell School of Art, where she became a prize-winning pupil of Victor Pasmore. At this time she began to acquire the marvellous technical facility and control later put to work in the Brazilian Amazon, though real plant painting was still to come.

In 1952, Margaret and Greville went to Brazil to look after her sister, Catherine, who was seriously ill. They settled in São Paulo, today Brazil's behemoth and the financial and industrial heart of the country, but in the early 1950s still relatively small and provincial. They settled down to a pleasant expatriate life, Margaret teaching art at St Paul's School, and Greville building up a commercial art business linked to the accelerating industrial development of the city.

It was here that Margaret discovered her métier as a plant portraitist. Like many another European visitor before her, she was overwhelmed by the beauty of the coastal forests of this area. Both Rio and São Paulo, Brazil's principal cities, grew up in what is today known as the Atlantic Forest. The most impressive part of this vegetation is that which grows on the granite "Sugar Loaf" mountains that range along the fringe of the ocean like some fantastic bulwark of fable. Even as late as the 1950s they were mostly still covered with beautiful and enchanting forests, described so many times by visiting naturalists in the nineteenth century. Being montane slope forests for the most part, subject to dense mists by night, they are extremely rich in epiphytes and ferns - many of the world's best-known ornamental plants were first collected there. The diversity of form and species is easily visible and the dramatic topography heightens the impression of a fantastic landscape. Even today the traveller may experience this in the now-protected forests of the Serra do Mar. We know today that this forest is one of the planet's richest genetic stores of biodiversity, and scientific knowledge of its biological riches is still incomplete. São Paulo lies on the plateau behind the coastal mountain range, and Margaret, Greville, and their Dutch friend Rita de Pagter often hiked from the city into the forested hills and vales. Margaret began to focus her work on plant portraits, and soon her adventurous spirit was drawn to the challenge of the Amazon, the mightiest tropical forest of them all, rich in plants, magical in romance and a magnet for the bold and the brave.

Her first journey to Amazonia, a shoestring affair with Rita, took place in 1956 when Margaret was already 46. With this journey she embarked on her true career. At an age when many people would be more concerned with their pension prospects, she began a risky and adventurous new life with all the eager enthusiasm of an eighteen-year-old. Whatever the eccentricity of two European ladies burying themselves in a spider-infested hut in a remote corner of the eastern Amazon, clearly a phenomenon new to the local inhabitants, the experience was a crucial one. On Margaret's return to São Paulo, her work advanced apace and the ensuing exhibitions at the Botanical Institute of São Paulo, in Rio de Janeiro in 1958 and in London in 1960 established her as a remarkable new botanical artist. The Rio exhibition was organized by her friend Professor Luiz Emygdio Mello Filho, Director of the National Museum of Brazil, who made the crucial introduction to Roberto Burle Marx, who was to become a particularly good friend. She was also noticed by Dr Alcides Teixeira, the Director of the Botanical Institute of São Paulo, his colleagues Dr Moisés Kuhlmann and Dr Oswaldo Handro, and Dr Lyman Smith, the world authority on bromeliads from Washington's Smithsonian Institution, who recognized in her the artist required for an important project, the Flora Brasilica.

The flora of Brazil is almost certainly the richest of any one nation on the planet. Nobody knows how many species of plant inhabit this vast land - recent estimates range from 55,000 to 65,000 - possibly one fifth of all plants. During the nineteenth century the German botanist Karl von Martius organized an international team, with the sponsorship of Emperor Dom Pedro II of Brazil, to write the flora of Brazil; it was completed in 1906, with some 23,000 species. This monumental botanical endeavour has not been surpassed in size or quality of production, but by 1940, another botanist, this time Brazilian, took up the challenge once again. Dr Frederico Carlos Hoehne, the extraordinarily energetic founder of the São Paulo Botanical Institute, began the Flora Brasilica, intended to be a revision of Martius' great work. Lyman Smith had already been working for many years on the flora of Brazil, and particularly on the family Bromeliaceae, which has its centre of diversity in the Atlantic Forest. A volume of bromeliads for the Flora Brasilica was therefore planned, with Margaret's paintings as the magnificent illustrations, one full folio plate for each species. Thus it was that she took up post in the Institute in 1960 as a resident botanical artist, and began to travel throughout Brazil in search of suitable subjects. Working side-by-side with a botanical authority of the stature of Lyman Smith meant that Margaret rapidly acquired a specialist knowledge of bromeliads and a particular brilliance in depicting them. Later, in the Amazon, with her by then experienced field botanist's eye, she discovered various new species, *Aechmea polyantha, Aechmea meeana, Neoregelia margaretae, Neoregelia leviana* and *Neoregelia meeana*, three of which were named after her. During the five years of the Flora Brasilica bromeliads project, Margaret met and became known and admired by many other botanists; in the dry northeastern states of Ceará and Pernambuco, she worked alongside the towering presence of Dr Dárdano de Andrade Lima, the region's pre-eminent botanist, collecting her bromeliads in the frazzling heat of the caatinga and mountain forests of the interior.

Unfortunately the project was not completed owing to shortage of funds for printing, and Lyman Smith was forced to look for another solution. In 1969, thirty two of these paintings were published in small format and of rather poor quality, which did not do justice to the originals (Lyman B. Smith & Margaret Mee, The Bromeliads, A.S. Barnes, South Brunswick and New York,

1969). Happily this was recently put right, when the entire collection of fifty-nine bromeliad paintings was published in a good quality edition by the Institute of Botany in São Paulo, in collaboration with the Margaret Mee Botanical Foundation of Brazil and with financial support from the Banco do Estado de São Paulo (Banespa). This collection gives an excellent insight into how widely Margaret travelled and collected at this period, with portraits of bromeliads from, among others, the northeastern states of Ceará and Pernambuco (1961), the southern state of Santa Catarina (1962), the centre of the continent in northern Mato Grosso (1963), the Rio Uaupés of the northwestern Amazon (1964), and many from localities in the environs of São Paulo and Rio de Janeiro such as Caraguatatuba, the Biological Station at Paranapiacaba, the mountains of Itatiaia and Campos do Jordão, the Organ Mountains and around the old colonial port of Paraty.

In this period, Margaret came to know her Brazil in the round, and her botanical knowledge advanced by leaps and bounds as she deepened her friendships with such botanical luminaries as Dr Kuhlmann, Pabst and Graziela Barroso, the latter particularly revered for her inspired teaching and leadership. These scientists, with their experience of the flora of this gigantic treasurehouse of biological diversity, widened Margaret's horizons and welcomed her enthusiastically into their circle. Roberto Burle Marx also became an increasingly important influence, particularly through their common and growing concern for the future conservation of the natural habitats by which they were both so fascinated. By the mid-Sixties the so-called "economic miracle" of Brazil was in full swing, and its implications for the forests were beginning to become worryingly clear. By the end of the bromeliad project in São Paulo she was becoming increasingly focused on the Amazon and felt the need for a change. In 1968, at Roberto Burle Marx's urging and encouraged by Prof. Luiz Emygdio Mello Filho, she and Greville decided to take the plunge and moved to Rio where they established themselves at the house in Santa Teresa. They were well placed for the Botanic Garden and even better for Roberto's studio in Laranjeiras just down the hill. Only a few streets away was Pabst's Herbarium Bradeanum, a private botanical institute, the nerve centre for studies of Brazilian orchids and bromeliads - the latter in the hands of Edmundo Pereira. Pabst was a man of exceptional energy and clearly saw a soul-mate in Margaret. Besides being a Vice President of the national airline, VARIG, he directed the Herbarium Bradeanum with verve and élan, building it up into a botanical institute of international repute, and still found time for plant explorations. His crowning work was the *Orchidaceae Brasilienses*, a book which described and illustrated all that was then known of Brazil's orchids, and with a painting by Margaret featured on the cover of each of the two volumes.

Margaret's fifteen journeys to the Amazon are described in magnificent style in "Margaret Mee - In Search of Flowers of the Amazon Forests," edited by Tony Morrison, where her adventures are recounted in detail. She developed a particular affection for the Rio Negro region, in the northwest part of Brazilian Amazonia and it was there that she made her final trip, in 1988, with Tony Morrison, Sally Duchess of Westminster, Sue Loram, Brian Sewell and Gilberto Castro, to paint the night-flowering "Moonflower" cactus (*Strophocactus wittii*). During these years of Amazon travels she established herself as an explorer of a very special kind, treated as an equal by others who, fired by different missions, had trodden the same wild paths through this, one of the world's mightiest wildernesses. Occasionally she would cross paths with Ghillean Prance, then leading

Amazonian botanical exploration for the New York Botanical Garden; she bumped into Robin Hanbury-Tenison during his cross-Amazonia dash, and with her knowledge and experience, was able to offer useful advice on fuel supplies and pilots in the depths of the forest. From the first she became involved with the Amerindian peoples of the Amazon, and her commitment to their cause became a dominating preoccupation as the years wore on. Equally passionate was her concern for the preservation of the Amazon forest and its wildlife. This led her to outspoken public statements during a period of Brazilian history when such activities could give rise to serious consequences. Side by side, she and Roberto Burle Marx succeeded in bringing these issues to the attention of many people both within Brazil and abroad. It is a measure of the enormous affection and esteem in which she was - and is still - held by Brazilian people that this has had no ill effects. President Geisel opened her 1977 exhibition in Brasília and later she was awarded the Brazilian decoration of the Order of the Southern Cross.

By the mid 1980s Margaret was becoming concerned to preserve her work as a permanent public record of what she was increasingly convinced was a vanishing world. For many years she had sold her original paintings as a means of earning a living, but she began to hold them back with the specific aim of building an Amazon Collection, which, she hoped, would one day be entrusted to an institution capable of making her paintings permanently available to the public. In vain she looked for opportunities to sell her collection, as donating it was unrealistic given their limited resources. With the advancing years, Margaret and Greville's thoughts would often turn to retirement in Britain. The sale of the Amazon Collection - now comprising 60 paintings, became a major preoccupation. At this time too, Margaret began to develop the technique of painting forest backgrounds to some of her plant portraits thus adding tremendously to their popular appeal. After many unavailing attempts to interest purchasers, a chink of light came with the entrance on the scene of the Hon. Christopher McLaren. During a trip to Brazil, he was so impressed by Margaret's work that he returned to the UK convinced of the need to secure the collection for posterity. Through his persistence, the Royal Botanic Gardens, Kew began to consider the question, but shortage of funds remained an apparently insuperable obstacle.

Thus it was that in January 1988, on another trip to Rio, I found myself once again drinking tea at the Mee's, this time with Tony Morrison, who was working with Margaret on the book of her diaries. Tony had the idea that what was needed was a Trust of some kind, which could organize and carry through a fund-raising campaign. The Amazon was much in the news, the time seemed ripe and success possible and he had contacts in London who he felt sure would help. By this time, Margaret's work had become part of Brazil's national heritage in the minds of many, and she herself was now a figure of national significance - if it should be that the Amazon Collection would eventually come to Kew, it was imperative that this move had to be balanced by a Brazilian element of at least equal weight. Margaret enthusiastically took up my suggestion for a scholarship scheme for young Brazilian botanical artists and botanists. Thus the germ of the Margaret Mee Amazon Trust was born. Back in London, Tony secured the ready agreement of Sir William Harding, a former British Ambassador to Brazil, to lead the Trust, and with Kew's backing in the person of Grenville Lucas, and with Christopher McLaren's energy and foresight, the Trust was soon in existence and the fund-raising campaign begun. A furiously active few months ensued during which many of Margarets old friends eagerly came forward to help: Sally Duchess of Westminster, Aylmer Tryon, John Hemming, The Hon. David Bigham, Marion Morrison, Ray Harley, the Earl of Dartmouth, Roberto Burle Marx and Richard Evans Schultes, among others, were soon involved. There was a most felicitous coincidence in the Trust's launch and the beginning of Ghillean Prance's Directorship of Kew; his wholehearted support gave a tremendous boost to the campaign. In November 1988 Margaret's book with Tony Morrison was published, and the Trust was officially launched at the preview of her Amazon Exhibition at Kew. Margaret gave an electrifying lecture at the Royal Geographical Society to a packed house, then made a whistle-stop tour to the US to promote the Nonesuch Expeditions book, and appeared on the McNeil-Lehrer show. Despite her 79 years, Margaret took everything in her stride, she seemed radiantly energetic and her message was getting through everywhere. At this exciting moment, disaster struck. Margaret was killed in a car accident. It seemed so ironic - after so many risks and dangers in the wilds of Amazonia, to be suddenly taken from us in domesticated middle England.

When the news reached Brazil, the reaction was immediate and the welcoming party planned for the Brazilian launch of her book became a moving commemorative gathering of tribute. Against the backdrop of a show of her paintings, attended by friends and former colleagues, the idea of a local Margaret Mee Botanical Foundation was launched.

Under the dynamic leadership of Philip Jenkins, the Fundação Botânica Margaret Mee came into being, buoyed up by tremendous support from people all over Brazil, but particularly Mário Gibson Barbosa, Luiz Emygdio Mello Filho, Joaquim Aurélio Nabuco, Sylvia de Botton Brautigam, Elizabeth Wynn-Jones, William Searight, Annie Phillips, Karen Vliegers, Sue Loram and Bob Broughton. Everyone was linked by the conviction that Margaret's spirit should live on, in fighting for Amazon conservation, in continuing her own adventurous approach to botanical illustration, in encouraging and stimulating young people, especially young Brazilians, to take up the enormous challenge posed by the Amazon's future, and in educating the public about the plant treasures of Amazonia through the superb medium of Margaret's paintings.

The work of the Trust and the Fundação over the ensuing 8 years has been and continues to be very successful in these aims. The funds to purchase Margaret's paintings, diaries and sketchbooks were raised, and they are now in the care of Kew, and are made available to the public at every suitable opportunity. Over one hundred and eighteen grants have been given to young Brazilian illustrators and biologists, to support their work in the Amazon and in the Atlantic Forest, where Margaret first perfected her vision of Brazilian plants. The Fundação has had a tremendous success in promoting Margaret's work in exhibitions, publications, training courses and events throughout Brazil. The link with the botanical community of Brazil is strong and lasting and the Fundação has a special place every year in the National Botanical Congress, where the Margaret Mee Prize is offered to the most promising young botanical artist of the year. Thirty three students have been awarded major scholarships to Great Britain, the majority working at Kew, where the Margaret Mee Amazon Trust is based.

Today the issues remain as urgent as during Margaret's lifetime. Amazonia is still by far the largest tract of tropical forest on the planet. Its future is uncertain, and the pressures are many. The evidence piling up clearly shows it to be a natural system of the utmost importance to our physical and biological future. But the human dilemma becomes ever more acute as economic, political, and national issues have to be addressed too. Amazonia is the stage on which an enormous and terrifying drama will be acted out over the coming decades: its outcome cannot be clearly discerned. Margaret Mee played a significant part in this drama, and we know that her work and spirit will live on in the inspiration and energy of new generations of young scientists and artists, their works and in her own superb paintings. Whatever may be the destiny of her beloved Amazon, future generations, thanks to Margaret, will inherit a true vision of the magic and beauty and breathtaking biological complexity of their wildwood past.

Simon Mayo, 10th September 1996, Kew.

Margaret Mee - The Artist

Brinsley Burbidge

We all have days which are etched indelibly into our memories by strong emotions. I remember, so clearly, the afternoon when Gail Bromley, a long-time friend of Margaret Mee and a colleague of mine at Kew, told me that Margaret had been killed in a car accident. The shock I felt was heightened by the fact that I had been part of the team which had put together Kew's first exhibition in the Kew Gardens Gallery showing a wide range of her wonderful paintings to a London audience for the first time. The exhibition had opened only a few days earlier, and we were all living in the euphoria of excellent exhibition reviews, proud of the fact that we had brought one of the world's outstanding painters and conservationists to Kew. The shock was made worse by the knowledge that the decision to hold the exhibition had brought Margaret to London and had shortened the life of someone I had grown to respect and admire.

Though I had known the work of Margaret Mee through reproductions for many years, I did not meet her until 1987. That meeting at Kew began an all too brief association with a truly remarkable woman. The frail, rather nervous, diffident, almost bird-like person of first acquaintance didn't match the tales of expeditions and adventure in Amazonian rainforest. The knowledge that her painting kit contained a .32 revolver didn't fit. Her fragility seemed at odds with the stories of malaria and hepatitis, of encounters with belligerent Indians, of near drownings, and of accidents which left her with broken ribs. And her reputation as a forceful and tireless campaigner against the indifference which permitted the destruction of the rainforest seemed at variance with the shy, attractive and hesitant seventy-five year old I first met. First impressions are often deceptive, and sheer physical strength is not always a prerequisite for Amazon explorers. Margaret's inner strength and determination to paint what she loved - the plants of the rainforest - together with her concern for the Amazon and its peoples quickly replaced any concern for her robustness. She was an intrepid explorer, as tough as they come, driven by a passion which made her unstoppable until a car on an English motorway did what the so-called hostile tropics could not do.

Her paintings, always direct from nature and always executed in the field, are some of the finest records of plants and their environments ever made. Let us begin by looking at the botanical illustration tradition of which she was such an important part.

Botany and illustration have always gone hand in hand. Some of the earliest recognizable drawings of plants were executed to permit searchers after cures for diseases to identify those species which would help. From the fifteenth century onward, botanical artists were employed to illustrate herbals - books which catalogued the medicinal value of plants - and illustration as a record or to facilitate identification has been at the heart of botanical illustration ever since.

Otis Imboden/National Geographic Image Collection

Margaret Mee sketching a bromeliad during her 1967 expedition to the
Pico da Neblina, the highest mountain peak on the upper Rio Negro

The rapid rise of scientific botany in the seventeenth and eighteenth centuries, coupled with
increasingly sophisticated methods of book production and printing, liberated botanical painting.
The rise of a wealthy merchant class, allied with an increasing enthusiasm for gardening, led to a
growing demand for books of plant pictures. The result of these demands was botanical painting
as a profession: illustrators were needed and the seventeenth, eighteenth and nineteenth centuries
produced a wealth of wonderful paintings in many media aimed at two rather distinct audiences.

The first of these was the world of science and horticulture. The demands it made were simple
and uncompromising: a fully accurate, representational picture of a plant to permit its precise
identification. Every petal, leaf and stamen must be exactly as it was on the plant, colors must be
faithful to nature: cold, clinical precision was everything. In most cases, the plant was illustrated
against a pure white background with not a hint of the plant's connection with nature. Even the
roots were washed free of soil. The only liberty permitted, the only artistic license allowed was,
curiously, for the artist to "repair" an insect-chewed leaf and make the plant even more perfect,

even more super-real than it was in life. The products are the true, pure botanical illustrations. Truth and purity, of course, do not always ostracize beauty. Many of the scientific illustrations produced for this demanding audience have immense charm and often have great pictorial qualities. Many are beautiful because of the strict demands made on the illustrator.

The bulk of Margaret's phenomenal output falls in the scientific illustration category and obeys the strict demands of the tradition. Everything is shown as it is in nature - all that is missing is the background. Scientists and gardeners love her paintings as they would a picture of an old friend. In many ways the picture is equivalent to the plant and can substitute for it. It is very rare for a botanist to fail to identify the species of plant in one of her paintings because some feature is not visible. Margaret spent much of her life with professional botanists, and she knew what they wanted. Perhaps the best known and best loved of her pictures are those of orchids, a plant family to which she gave particular attention and which she painted with consummate mastery.

If Margaret had only painted accurate representations of plants, her work would have been significant. But she did a great deal more. Her innate ability as an artist, sharpened by her time at art college learning from various artists including Victor Pasmore, co-founder along with Claude Rogers and William Coldstream of the Euston Road Group, enabled her to produce superbly satisfying compositions. In fact, it is often the composition that you notice first after admiring the beauty of the plant. Surprisingly, even though she had always drawn and painted, it was not until she was almost forty that she took the formal lessons which turned her latent talent into a mature fluidity in which everything she did, even the humblest study, had style and elegance.

I have briefly mentioned the two audiences for pictures of plants and discussed Margaret's ability to satisfy only one of them - the scientific and horticultural fraternity. The other audience wanted beauty alone and was not at all concerned with accuracy. We are, here, in the world of painting rather than illustration and the product provided by the artist to satisfy this want became known as the flower painting or the flower piece. Going back again to seventeenth century Europe, especially Holland, a demand came from wealthy merchants to have flower pictures on their walls in winter which substituted for the flowers which bloomed in their gardens in summer. This led to a vast outpouring of talent into the production of still life paintings in which flowers featured very heavily and began a tradition which continues to this day. The French Impressionists made their own outstanding contribution to flower painting, and contemporary artists continue to see flowers as great subjects for paintings. What has all this got to do with Margaret Mee - a veteran of fifteen Amazonian expeditions and an associate of botanists?

The answer lies in some of her extraordinary paintings which show plants against a pictorial backdrop. They fit right into the flower painting tradition and can hold their own with the best of the Dutch or French painters - but there is one significant difference: in all of Margaret's paintings, you can identify the plants in the foreground and background. Her scientific imperative has won through, but has left us with something which could hang with full confidence in the company of paintings by Van Huysum, Ruysch, Van Os, Monet, Renoir and Georgia O'Keefe. It is very obvious that I rank her among the greatest botanical illustrators of all time: with these few names, I also put her firmly in the world of great artists.

Though I adore her paintings, I am captivated and enchanted by her studies and sketchbook. It is here that we see Margaret at work, and we are very fortunate that these are an important part of this exhibition. For some reason, Margaret's studies have a completeness and an integrity which set them apart from many other studies. Even though many have only one petal or one leaf in full color, even though some parts are only hinted at or are shown in outline, she still seems to have worked on them until they felt right. Her instinct for composition compels her to go on until the composition, however slender, works. Each study is a perfect work of art in its own right. Very little exists in the way of published material that gives a critical review of Margaret's work.

Little has also been published on the way Margaret worked except for the fact that she worked in gouache as a medium, rather than the more traditional watercolor. I find this neglect of technique significant. Technique is important to other painters who want to learn from her work and emulate what she has done, but to most of us, it is incidental or even irrelevant. Margaret was a painter who knew how to use her talents and her tools to create something which worked. She was always willing to discuss technique with other painters, but somehow treated it with the same enthusiasm that she would give to a discussion on paddling a canoe: it was a means to an end. Enjoy her wonderful orchids, marvel at her stunning bromeliads and fall in love with the pictures and the flowers they represent. Beyond this, be concerned that they and the world they inhabit are threatened with extinction and think what you can do to help. She would have wanted that.

Conservation of the Amazon Rainforest

Ghillean T. Prance

When Margaret Mee first visited the Amazon region in 1956, she visited a pristine environment that inspired her beautiful paintings of Amazonian plants. However, the 1960's were different as Brazil began to develop the region, build the Trans-Amazon highway, and later encourage the establishment of large cattle ranches. The period of Margaret's expeditions to Amazonia between 1956 and 1988 coincided with the period of maximum deforestation in the region, especially in the 1970's and 1980's. It is, therefore, hardly surprising that someone like Margaret Mee, with an activist background and a special love for the Amazon forest, became one of its foremost defenders. This was during the years of a military regime in Brazil where it was not fashionable to criticize government policy. However, the opinions of this remarkable, elegant and fragile-looking artist were tolerated, listened to and effective in raising concern, both within Brazil and overseas. So much so, that the military President of Brazil, General Geisel, opened her 1977 exhibition in the capital city of Brasília.

Margaret's concern for the Amazon environment is reflected in her later paintings, where she added a forest background to her plant portraits. In these later paintings, she tried to show that the plants she studied and painted depended upon the whole habitat for their survival. Since Margaret was one of the first and most courageous defenders of the Amazon rainforest, it is most appropriate that a short essay on the conservation of the region be included in this catalogue.

The conservation of the Amazon rainforest will only be achieved through a balance between biological conservation in reserves, National Parks, indigenous areas and other conservation units and sustainable-use projects. I will, therefore, cover aspects of both these issues, because the one cannot be isolated from the other. The World conservation Strategy, published in 1980 by IUCN, UNEP and WWF, began to suggest the merging of the interests of conservation and utilization and much progress has been made over the intervening period. The Convention on Biological Diversity, appropriately drafted at the Rio de Janeiro Earth Summit of 1992 in Margaret Mee's home city, emphasized both conservation of biodiversity and the sustainable use of its components.

1. Tropical Forest

In order to consider conservation and utilization of tropical rainforest, it is important to understand a few basic features of this ecosystem that make it different from other ecosystems and present special problems to the conservation planner and the developer alike.

a. Diversity

Tropical rainforest is the most species-diverse ecosystem in the world and it is an Amazonian forest that holds the record for number of tree species of 10cm diameter or more on a hectare of forest: 300 species/Ha at Yanomono in Peru, according to the work of the late Alwyn Genty, another Amazonian pioneer explorer.

Quantitative inventories that have been carried out through the Amazon vary from 80 to 300 trees per hectare. In addition, there is a rich flora of herbs, shrubs and epiphytes. With a tree diversity of this magnitude, there are not many individuals of any single species on a hectare. Many species are represented by a single individual in all terra firme rainforest quantitative inventories which I have carried out. To the biologist, and to an artist like Margaret Mee, this is the wonder of the Amazon forest and the compelling reason for its preservation. To the developer, diversity is the problem. The useful species that he wants to exploit are dispersed widely among all the other trees. It is easier to fell the forest and create a monoculture of a timber plantation or a cattle pasture.

b. Vegetational Diversity

The myth that the Amazon rainforest is one homogenous type has long been dispelled. All more recent surveys and maps have shown that many different types of vegetation exist in an elaborate mosaic throughout the region. The vegetation map of Venezuela, prepared by Huber and Alarcon in 1988, contains 150 categories of vegetation, many of which occur within the Amazon region, and the work of projeto RADAMBRASIL has shown how varied is the vegetation of Amazonian Brazil. Some of the major categories include forest on terra firme, várzea, igapó, Amazonian caatinga, savanna, babassu transitional forest and the bamboo forests of Acre. However, all these and the other major types of vegetation can be divided into many subdivisions. Each type of vegetation requires different methods of conservation and different techniques for sustainable management.

c. Soils

Edaphic factors are of particular importance in rainforest areas, because of the extent of poor soils under most of these forests. The soils are nutrient poor and do not have the colloidal properties to retain nutrients. The rainforest depends on its ability to recycle nutrients without loss. A leaf falls from a tree and it is soon connected to the roots of another tree by mycorrhizae. Trees have roots which seek out nutrient-rich areas, such as decaying logs. The soils of Margaret Mee's beloved Rio Negro region are particularly fragile, because of the large areas of white sand, which contain scarcely any nutrients and are covered by caatinga or savanna. The poor nature of the soils means that forest cover is by far the best land use. Therefore, both conservation and utilization programs must consider ways to maintain the forest and the delicate nutrient cycle. This means conservation of mycorrhizal fungi and of many soil organisms.

d. The Web of Interactions

The more the Amazon rainforest is studied, the more we are realizing the complexity of the interactions between the component organisms. I will mention two typical examples of such interactions.

The cabalash tree (*Crescentia cujete*) is the most important vessel in Amazonia, but in order to develop the fruit which forms the calabash, the work of a bat and of ants is essential. The green flowers which are borne on the branches are pollinated by bats. The fruit begins to develop, but while they are young, they are soft and would be subject to predation if it were not for the hoards of aggressive ants that sip the nectar produced by extrafloral nectaries all over the surface of the young fruit. As the fruit expands to the size of a football, the nectaries dry up, the ants depart and the outer shell becomes hard and woody and is therefore mechanically protected from predators. The ants perform their defensive function through the crucial stage of development of the fruit.

The Brazil nut (*Bertholletia excelsa*) is also an important economic plant of the Amazon forest. The nut crop is almost entirely harvested from wild trees. The large yellow flowers, with a complicated structure, can only be pollinated by large bees that are able to lift the hood of the androecium to give access to the nectar. The most common pollinator is a large Euglossine, or orchid bee (*Eulaema meriana*). This been depends on various large-flowered species, or orchids, such as *Cattleya* and *Stanhopea*, to gather fragrance which it packs into special pockets in the hind legs, to attract female bees for mating. Brazilnuts are borne in a hard woody fruit about the size of a baseball, which takes 14-16 months to develop after pollination and then falls to the forest floor from the canopy of these 40-50 foot tall trees. The only animal with teeth strong enough to gnaw open the fruit capsule and remove the nuts is the agouti (*Dasyprocta*). The agouti store the nuts in buried hoards away from the parent tree and are thus the dispersal agent of these seeds. To produce and maintain one of the most important extraction crops of the Amazon rainforest, the presence of a bee, an orchid and an agouti are essential. Such is the network that weaves together the different organisms of a rainforest. Conservation planning must include knowledge about interactions. The conservation of a single species will seldom work, because of its dependence on other parts of the web, and some keystone species are vital to any ecosystem.

2. Indigenous populations

Margaret Mee frequently visited indigenous tribal peoples for whom she had a great respect. Until recently, we have considered the Amazon rainforest to be relatively undisturbed. However, before the conquest by European civilization, the region was occupied by a substantial human population, the Amazon Indians. These people certainly cut forests for their clearings, and evidence of the extent of their occupation is seen in charcoal remnants in the soil. However, their system did not destroy the plant and animal species, nor the nutrient cycling process.

Recent studies of quantitative ethnobotany of contemporary Amazon forest dwellers have shown the extent to which indigenous peoples depend upon the forest. A study of the Chácobo Indians of Bolivia, by Brian Boom of the New York Botanical Garden, showed that they have a use for 82 percent of the species of trees (75 out of 91) in a sample hectare of forest. This included 95 percent of the individual trees (619 out of 649). A second study of the Kàapor Indians of Brazil, by William Balée, found that they had a use for every single species of tree in the sample hectare. The uses included food, fibres, construction materials, fuel, medicines, rubber latex, etc. If one depends upon the rainforest trees to that extent, it is not in one's interest to destroy it all for agriculture. Many Indian groups live by making small clearings and on extraction and hunting from the forest, but they seldom exploit the species to extinction.

3. Extraction

The Campesinos, or Caboclos, who now inhabit much of the Amazon region, have learned much from the Indians and also often make their living by extraction of products from the rainforest.

There are many products to be harvested from the rainforest that have market value. One of the first assessments of this was made by ecologist Charles Peters, working together with a botanist and economist, Robert Mendelsohn. They studied a hectare of species-diverse rainforest at Mishana, in the Peruvian Amazon, which contained 275 species of trees. Seventy-two of these species (26 percent), representing 350 of the 842 trees of ten centimeters in diameter or more, could yield products of monetary value in the market of the nearby town of Iquitos. These comprised edible fruit from 11 species, 2 species of Hevea rubber, and 60 species that yield locally commercial timber. The study calculated production rates of all the products, retail prices, and labor and transportation costs. The results indicated an estimated net present value (NPV) per hectare of natural forest of $6,820. This is contrasted with the NPV of a managed plantation of the pulp wood species Gmelina arborea on deforested land in Pará, Brazil, of $3,184/Ha, and of a good Amazonian cattle pasture in Venezuela of $2,960/Ha.

These and several other recent studies in Amazonia indicate that harvesting the standing rainforest of some areas makes sense, both ecologically and economically. This should be no surprise, because of the poor soils and delicate recycling system of nutrients in most rainforests, which render than unsuitable for conventional agriculture. Extraction will be one of the many alternative solutions for rainforest areas, but it will certainly not solve all the problems. To be a viable concept for conservation, considerable control needs to be exercised in extraction forests about what products and in what quantity they are harvested. This is particularly important for animals, which can easily be over-hunted. In order to be commercially viable, extraction must be based on diversity of products, because of the diversity of the forest. This means that rather small quantities of a large number of products are available. In today's economy, it is hard to develop small markets, rather than bulk markets. Products that need only small quantities to be effective, such as flavors and fragrances, have the greatest potential. The challenge before us now is to follow the example of the Indians and to find uses for many of the rainforest plants, and to work with industries that are willing to develop new products in line with the supply. There are certainly many untapped resources in the Amazon rainforest, such as resins, latex other than rubber, aromatic barks, fruits with exotic flavors, such as the relative of the cocoa bean, Cupuaçu (Theobroma grandiflorum), or the popular fruit in Pará, Brazil, the bacuri (Platonia insignis).

Some of the products that will be discovered in the process of extraction will also lend themselves to cultivation in mixed crop agroforestry systems, the other alternative for productive management of fragile Amazon soils. For example, the Cupuaçu cited above, is already being grown as a commercial crop, as well as an extraction product. The first large Brazilnut plantation near Itacoatiara, Brazil, promises to be successful, because it has utilized much of the available ecological information about that species.

Brazil has set up several extractivist reserves, especially in the States of Acre and Amapá, where rubber tappers and Brazilnut gatherers are permitted to extract products from the forest, but not to clear cut. There is no doubt that in some places this has slowed down the deforestation and has been a temporary solution. However, there are still many social problems and the extractivists eke out a meager existence, because of the low market value of their products. Estractivist reserves are unlikely to be a major permanent solution for conserving the forest.

4. Ecotourism

Tourism in the rainforest should certainly be part of conservation planning. The Amazon, with its variety of beautiful scenery and interesting plants and animals, especially lends itself to the possibilities of ecotourism. Tourists will pay a lot to see the forest, the animals and nature in general, but not to see cattle pasture or secondary forest. Tourism only combines with conservation when it is extremely well planned and rigorously controlled. Numbers must be limited to the amount that the ecosystem can take without pollution or other degradation. Limited tourism is one of the ways in which the rainforest can yield an income. This has worked well in Africa, and some of the tourist lodges in Amazonian Peru are an indication of what can be done in all of Amazonia.

5. Agroforestry

The economics quoted above, and many other examples, have shown that monoculture systems rarely work in areas that were formerly covered by rainforest. It is interesting to note that indigenous systems of agriculture are usually mixed-crop agroforestry, using a mixture of herbaceous and tree crops right from the initial planting. A regeneration cycle is started, which gradually turns a field into an extraction forest. Such systems have been studied in detail for the Kayapó Indians of Brazil, by Darrell Posey, the Huastec Mayans, by Janice Alcorn, and the Bora Indians of Peru. The example of the Bora Indians, shown in the figures taken from the work of Christine Padoch and William Denevan, shows this progression well. The nineteen-year-old forest, in Figure 1, is still visited by the Indians to harvest 22 useful species. This type of system has been adopted by various Peruvian riberiño communities, such as the village of Tamishiyacu, which was also studied by Christine Padoch. In that case, much of the area under use is now in the second phase of the 35-year cycle and some is already into the third. This study showed that an agroforestry system, quite similar to that of the Bora Indians, existed there. The succession from initial planting to forest and orchard continued for 35 years and was then felled and repeated. The skillful use of various components of the system was noted. One of the most marketable fruits, the umari (*Poraqueiba sericea*) was grown in small orchards, with a number of different varieties. At the completion of the cycle, this tree was used for charcoal, another marketable product. Brazilnut trees were also an important part of

Margaret Mee became an important outspoken advocate for the conservation of the Amazon, documenting the devastation with simple sketchbook drawings

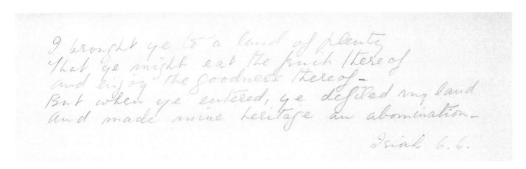

the system. At maturity, a few of these trees were cut to use and sell their timber, and others were left standing, in the new cycle to continue the production of Brazilnuts, which are not produced until a tree is at least 12 years of age. In addition to his productive agroforestry system on upland non-flooded ground, the Tamshiyaceños cultivate rice and beans on the floodplains of the river. These crops grow well there in annual cycles between the flood seasons. Alluvial matter enriches this soil, so that it can be used continuously. The most striking result of this study was that the 1987 income of a family of Tamshiyacu was just over $5,000, a remarkable amount anywhere in Peru.

Over two thousand miles distant from Tamshiyacu, Anthony Anderson and his team studied the economy of the Amazon estuary caboclos, who depend on the açaí palm (*Euterpe oleracea*) for their livelihood. These farmers extract the fruit pulp and heart-of-palm from açaí and manage the forest to maximize the number of useful plants. Table 1 shows the results of the study of a family on Ilha das Onças, near to the city of Belém. Again, this peasant farmer is gaining a sustainable income, without clear-cutting the forest.

The economic success of the two examples given above is not only due to their good ecology and sustainability, but also because Tamshiyacu and Ilha das Onças are near to the large city markets of Iquitos and Belém respectively. Other studies indicate that it is too costly to transport the type of goods produced in these systems over long distances. For example, Christine Padoch and Wil de Jong studied another Amazonian village, Santa Rosa, which is further from Iquitos. Although the annual market value of produce from a hectare was a possible $653, the owner actually realized only $22 in cash. However, much of the production was consumed locally by the farmer and his extended family. Another problem with the systems that work well is their long-term stability, simply because economic success brings progress to the people. As education increases, so willingness to stay on the land decreases.

6. Conservation

The whole Amazon Basin must not be turned into extraction reserves, agroforestry systems and tourist areas but a balance between conservation and sustainable utilization is needed. In this, selection of areas as biological reserves is of crucial importance. These must not be based on areas that are unsuitable for other uses, but on biological criteria, such as centers of diversity and endemism. A large step forward in this process was made in Workshop 90, held in Manaus, Brazil, in January 1990. This meeting brought together 100 biologists to pool their data about the priority areas for conservation, based on their biogeographical knowledge of the region. The result was a map with five levels of conservation priority that indicated 53 percent of the Amazon region of particular importance for conservation (Fig. 2). This included most of the Venezuelan Amazon. The process was based entirely on biological information and not on actual land use of ground. True data and the actual selection of reserves will need a lot more work.

Historic Riverine Journeys
Plant Hunting along the Amazon and its Tributaries

Ruth L. A. Stiff

As the Amazon River wends its way four thousand miles across the South American continent, through the largest and most majestic forest on earth, it carries one fifth of the earth's fresh water to the oceans of the world. This incomparable natural resource, with its wealth of flora and fauna of dazzling complexity amid its mosaic of massive tributaries, forests, savannas, and flood plains, has been the scene of some of the most extraordinary riverine journeys in the history of exploration.

From as early as 1495, there are documented voyages along the eastern coast of South America. However, it was on April 22, 1500 A.D., that Pedro Álvares Cabral of Portugal, commander of thirteen ships and 1200 men, first sighted the coast of Brazil and it is to him that history accords the discovery of this extraordinary land. Incredibly enough, for more than three hundred years after its discovery, Brazil remained essentially closed to the outside scientific world. The rivalry between Spain and Portugal, the two major exploratory nations of this period, together with European wars and local politics, conspired to keep travel within the country limited and provincial.

Elsewhere in South America, scientific expeditions of European origin gained in prominence during the eighteenth century. Charles Marie de La Condamine commenced an expedition to Peru in 1735 to conduct triangulation experiments on the equator to ascertain the shape of the earth. To the north in Venezuela, the Prussian Baron Alexander von Humboldt arrived with the French botanist Aimé Jacques Alexandre Bonpland in 1799 to explore the river Orinoco. Their highly successful expedition culminated with the confirmation of the existence of the remarkable Casiquiare Canal, a unique natural waterway navigable for 140 miles which flows in two directions, connecting the Orinoco, flowing northward into Venezuela, and the Rio Negro, flowing southeast into Brazil. In addition, the fruits of their labors resulted in the collection of an astounding 12,000 specimens of plants, producing what is now known as the most complete data base ever having been compiled of this area.

The year 1808 ushered in a new era for Brazil, as the ports were opened to international commerce and foreign travelers. Nine years later, the Austrian Karl Friedrich Philipp von Martius and his zoologist companion Johann Baptist von Spix, commenced a three year journey throughout the eastern states of Brazil and Amazonia, initiating the production of what is arguably the largest flora ever published, the *Flora Brasiliensis*. This monumental work, intended as a record of all the known plants of Brazil, was published over a span of sixty-six years, from 1840 to 1906, with the first fifteen of thirty volumes contributed by Martius. An international team of sixty-five botanists and thirty-eight artists completed the work which encompassed nearly 23,000 species!

As extensive as this undertaking was, it still represented only a portion of the Brazilian flora. According to Professor Richard Schultes, Director Emeritus, Botanical Museum of Harvard University and a leading world authority on the ethnobotany of the Amazon Basin, the Amazon region alone may contain as many as 90,000 different plant species and, if the slopes of the Andes are included, possibly as many as 120,000.[1] Within this context, it can be readily understood that there was yet an immense task awaiting the next wave of naturalists.

The three most prominent figures in 19th century British exploration of Amazonia were the naturalists, Alfred Russel Wallace, Henry Walter Bates and Richard Spruce. Wallace and Bates arrived in Belém near the mouth of the Amazon river in the spring of 1848, over a year before Spruce. Their express purpose was:

> "to make for ourselves a collection of objects, dispose of the duplicates in London to pay expenses, and gather facts, as Mr. Wallace expressed in one of his letters, towards solving the problem of the origin of the species, a subject on which we have conversed and corresponded much together". [2]

Plagued by periods of ill-health, Wallace worked in the region for four years before returning to England in 1852. Bates remained a total of eleven years, exploring the entire valley of the Amazon where he collected more than 14,000 species of insects, of which 8,000 were previously unknown.

Under Bates's influence, Wallace, whose initial interest lay in trees, shrubs and flowers, developed a keen interest in entomology. Consequently, the majority of their scholarly writings, apart from Wallace's treatise *Palm Trees of the Amazon and their Uses* (1853), were about the fauna of the region, ensuring the two would be remembered largely as zoologists. Subsequently, both men made significant contributions to the theory of evolution. Bates's demonstration of the operation of natural selection in animal mimicry and Wallace's theory of the origin of the species through natural selection, (independent of Darwin) gave solid support to the theories of Charles Darwin. In addition, the journals of Wallace and Bates published respectively as *A Narrative of Travels on the Amazon and Rio Negro* (1853), and *The Naturalist on the River Amazons*, two volumes (1883), have become classics of travel literature.

Richard Spruce, one of the greatest plant explorers of all time, landed in Belém in 1849 to commence fifteen continuous years of arduous exploration. He traveled the entire length of the Amazon, the Rio Negro and across the Andes, representing some of the wildest regions of South America - "*some so inaccessible that only now, after more than 140 years, are they again being penetrated by botanists*".[3] Traveling through these remote and dangerous forests, he was often unaccompanied but took great interest in learning the way of life and customs of the local people, frequently earning their friendship with his humble, forthright manner and gentle humor.

As a naturalist-explorer, his field notebooks and extensive correspondence included meticulous notes on the gathering and cultivation of plants, native economic plants and ethnobotany, entomology, history, native languages, sociology, anthropology, and geology. In his careful script he gave a detailed description of all that he encountered, including his observations of the local people's understanding and usage of the natural products of the forest. He was, for example, one of the first to specify the techniques of rubber tapping and processing. (4) Furthermore, his collections in Amazonia provided the basis for descriptions of six new species of *Hevea*, the genus that comprises the most significant source of natural rubber. (5)

In 1859 Spruce received word that he had been commissioned by Her Majesty's Secretary of State for India to prospect for the *Cinchona* tree whose bark contains quinine, an alkaloid possessing anti-malarial properties. Enduring unspeakable hardships, Spruce traveled to the Ecuadorian Andes where he collected for three years, procuring seeds and living material of the best grades of *Cinchona*. Upon their arrival in India, these seeds were utilized for the creation of large plantations to provide quinine and combat malaria throughout the British colonies.

Spruce ultimately amassed a vast collection of over 7,000 species of plants, sent for identification to George Bentham, a distinguished botanist at the Royal Botanic Gardens, Kew, who then shared this material with prominent herbaria around the world. Professor Joseph Ewan, of the Missouri Botanical Garden, notes that *"today, forty-three herbaria hold priceless vestiges of species preserved by Spruce that in some instances have been exterminated in the wild, or teeter on the edge of extinction"*. (6) In addition to his herbarium specimens, Spruce sent numerous artifacts to Kew's Museum of Economic Botany which had opened in 1848, one year prior to his departure for Brazil. This material included items of apparel, weapons, ornaments, and instruments, and also samples of economic products such as fibres, fruits, gums, dyes, and timber.

In 1864 Spruce returned to England, having traveled and botanized across the entire continent of South America. Despite his delicate health, he worked steadily on his plant collections, composing scientific papers and books and corresponding with British and foreign specialists until his death in 1893. Spruce never achieved the fame of his fellow explorers primarily because his journals remained unpublished during his lifetime. Fifteen years after his death, Spruce's diaries entitled

Above: The indefatigable collector and explorer,

Richard Spruce 1817-1893   Trustees, Royal Botanic Gardnes, Kew

Notes of a Botanist on the Amazon and Andes (1908) were published, edited by his old friend and fellow explorer Alfred Russel Wallace.

Margaret Mee followed in this grand tradition of Amazonian exploration. Often referred to as the premier female explorer of the Brazilian rainforest, she was also an outstanding botanical artist, acclaimed worldwide by botanists and art critics alike. Arriving in Brazil from England in 1952 at the age of forty-three, she was initially drawn to the lush tropical flora of the southern coastal mountains, the Serra do Mar, where she began to paint the native bromeliads of the coastal forest. During this period she worked alongside Dr. Lyman Smith, an American botanist from the Smithsonian Institution who was studying bromeliads at the Instituto de Botânica de São Paulo. With Dr. Smith, Margaret Mee produced numerous paintings for a book on bromeliads. [7]

Four years later, however, the beauty and diversity of the great Amazon basin seemed to captivate her interest in much the same manner as it had affected Richard Spruce more than a century earlier. Over the next three decades, Margaret Mee made fifteen long and arduous journeys to Brazilian Amazonia to search for, collect and paint its magnificent plants, many of which were entirely new to science.

Her itineraries often followed those of Spruce. If one were to prepare a map overlay of Richard Spruce and Margaret Mee's journeys, one would readily see the extent to which they explored

Kew's Museum of Economic Botany, which opened in 1848, displayed a fascinating array of "curiosities" from around the world, including the numerous Amazonian artifacts brought back to England by Richard Spruce

common regions. Although they both traveled extensively throughout the Amazon, it was the Rio Negro that appeared to evoke their greatest interest. In writing the preface to Margaret Mee's diaries, published by Nonesuch Expeditions Ltd in 1988, Professor Schultes notes:

> "Of very special interest to me...is her dedication to the forests of the Rio Negro area. It was here also that one of the greatest, but one of the least appreciated explorers of all time, the Yorkshire botanist Richard Spruce spent five productive years more than a century ago. In a very real way, Margaret honoured Spruce's extraordinary contribution. For the two have much in common: She is shy and self-effacing, as was he; and both, without actually realizing the extent, have enriched our knowledge of the richest part of the Amazonian flora." (8)

Of Margaret Mee's fifteen journeys, nine were to the Rio Negro. For her, it was the richness of its beauty and the secrets still held by its great forests that drew her on. As Professor Sir Ghillean T. Prance, Director of the Royal Botanic Gardens, Kew, states so eloquently in the preface to her diaries:

> "The Rio Negro region of Amazonia has called to the artist in Margaret Mee, with a call insistent and persistent. The ephemeral beauty, the light and shadow, the reflectance of the water, the magic of an opening flower bud have summoned her to ignore the frailties of body, and so to face repeatedly the rigors and dangers of river journeys of Sprucean extension." (9)

Both Spruce and Mee explored the Arquipelago das Anavilhanas on their way up the Rio Negro. This area is characterized by a maze of islands and igapós, (naturally flooded forest) that extends to more than sixty miles upstream, with an estimated 500 islands. In his journals, Spruce described this area as follows:

> "In many places, the river spreads out to an enormous width. Frequently it is sprinkled with islands, and sometimes opens out into a lake-like expanse, so wide that were it not for the lofty skirting forest, the opposite coast would be invisible." (10)

From this region, Mee brought out a fine collection of plants that included the spectacular orchid *Cattleya violacea*, first discovered in the early 1800s on the Rio Orinoco by Humboldt and Bonpland, and subsequently collected by Spruce some fifty years later. It was also in this region of the Rio Negro that Mee found, after many years of searching, the night-flowering cactus *Selenicereus wittii*, of which each blossom opens at night for only one night. It is believed to be pollinated by long-tongued hawkmoths.

Both Mee and Spruce collected in the area of the upper Rio Negro as well. According to Spruce's journals, he set sail in November of 1851 for São Gabriel, a settlement which served as his collecting station for several months during the years 1852 and 1853. He considered this journey a very successful one, as during the two month voyage he dried some 3,000 specimens, a much greater number than he had ever dried on any previous voyage. He was particularly struck by *Heterostemon mimosoides*, which "*was in flower all the way up the river and formed a great ornament to its banks.*" (11) This legume was later collected by Margaret Mee, and she completed her painting of this plant in 1978.

Margaret Mee crossing a suspended log bridge during here 1967 expedition to the
Pico da Neblina

The striking rain forest tree, *Gustavia pulchra*, was first discovered by Richard Spruce, and in a letter to a colleague in London dated April 15, 1852, Spruce noted that *"Gustavias were tolerably frequent, [on the upper Rio Negro] but it was scarcely possibly to preserve their flowers on account of the number of caterpillars bred in them."* (12) This plant was also collected and sketched by Margaret Mee in 1979.

The area surrounding São Gabriel is quite mountainous, and both Margaret Mee and Richard Spruce expressed attraction to these mysterious peaks, describing them as huge masses of granite rising abruptly out of the plains. The main peak in this area is the Pico da Neblina, which Spruce sighted in the summer of 1853. Writing to Sir William Hooker at Kew he noted: *"I could distinctly see, though at a great distance, The Serrania, called Pirá-pukú, or the long fish".* (13) Spruce never reached these mountains and it was not until 1953, exactly 100 years later, that a team of botanists and explorers from the New York Botanical Garden, together with Venezuelan explorers, made the first recorded ascent of this mountain. The entire massif was named the Cerro da Neblina, 'Mountain of Mist', and its height of 9,985 feet was duly recorded.

Financed by the National Geographic Society, Margaret Mee became the first woman traveler to attempt the southern approach to this mountain. Unfortunately, the "Mountain of Mist" proved true to its name. Torrential rainfall totally obliterated the path and it became impossible to reach the summit. A new trail would have taken weeks, if not months, to create. Mee wrote, *"I was bitterly disappointed and could not restrain my tears".* (14) The report of their 1967 expedition, with a list of species collected, including one new species, a bromeliad *Neoregelia leviana*, was published in the National Geographic Society Research Reports.

The Rio Uaupés, a tributary of the upper Rio Negro, was an area extensively explored by both Richard Spruce and Margaret Mee, albeit a century apart. Mee spent two months in this area on her third journey in 1964. Both Mee and Spruce report finding a wealth of interesting plants. During this expedition she painted, among other plants, the beautiful bignonia *Distictella magnolifolia*, first discovered by Humboldt in the early 1800's, and the unusual plant *Raputea paludosa*, which she described as *"an extraordinary swamp plant".* (15)

Spruce spent six and a half months along this river. His uncanny ability to search out rare plants was evidenced very clearly during this time. In a letter to Sir William Hooker dated June 27, 1853, he wrote that of his collection of some 500 species from this area, approximately four-fifths were as yet undescribed. It was here in 1852 that Spruce first discovered the lovely *Clusia grandifolia* which was subsequently collected and sketched by Mee in this same area in 1983.

Both Spuce and Mee were disappointed to have to leave this region. Mee felt that her time to leave came too soon and expressed a hope that one day she would return to explore this *"region of enchanting beauty".*(16) Spruce was even more prolific in his praise, though it was laced with a touch of nostalgia:

> *"I well recollect how the banks of the river became clad with flowers, as it were by some sudden magic, and how I said to myself, as I scanned the lofty trees with wistful and disappointed eyes, 'there goes a new Dipteryx, there goes a new Qualea - there goes a new the Lord knows what', until I could no longer bear the sight, and covering up my face with*

my hands, I resigned myself to the sorrowful reflection that I must leave all these fine things 'to waste their sweetness on the desert air'." [17]

These two intrepid travelers shared not only common paths and pursuits, but suffered many of the same adversities as well. On their respective voyages on the Rio Negro, Richard Spruce and Margaret Mee often encountered unpredictable weather. In his journals, Spruce noted: *"There is no foretelling the weather on the Rio Negro. When one looks for fair weather cometh rain, and the contrary."*[18] Mee's diary entry from her fifth journey seems to echo Spruce's words: *"The wind blew up suddenly as it does in a matter of seconds on the Negro - on other rivers, it never seems to break so quickly."* [19]

Rapids or cataracts were another hazard of the upper Rio Negro which caused much distress to both Spruce and Mee alike, endangering weeks of hard labor by threatening to drench dry specimens and wash away cuttings and plantings so carefully preserved. Margaret Mee described these difficult passings as follows:

"...The boat had to be lifted over the rocks and dragged through the ragging torrent. It took over an hour to pass the first fall, with much sweating and straining. The only way up was among the rocks near the bank and the two Indians used long poles to lever the hull across the obstruction which took until midday to pass." [20]

Spruce described a similar situation in more detail:

"I took the helm, though very ill-disposed for the task. The pilot leaped into the water with two or three more, applying their shoulders to the canoe, whilst the rest on board lugged at a rope made fast on shore beyond the point. In our course lay a sunken rock, which it was thought the canoe might pass; but instead, she struck on it and immediately fell over on one side, The boat swung around, forcing the rope out of the hands of the men, who instantly leaped into the water, and I was left alone, I stuck pertinaciously to the helm. The canoe again swung round and fell over on the contrary side, and all thought this time she would have gone clean over; but she did not. Another revolution and she swung fairly off the rock, righting at the same time. I set her head to the fall and she shot down like an arrow." [21]

They both became dangerously ill as a result of their travels - Spruce with malaria and numerous unidentified debilitating 'fevers', and Mee with malaria and infectious hepatitis. Both were given up for dead. Each in turn suffered from exhaustion, severe hunger, and inhospitable accommodations where they encountered, among other things, the nightly attacks of vampire bats. Calling them *"those midnight blood-letters"*, [22] Spruce noted that there were large patches of dried blood on the floor caused by the nightly strikes on the finger ends, noses, chins and toes of unsuspecting victims while they slept. Mee sympathised more than once with Spruce's complaints. Her diary entry written in August of 1967 reads as follows: *"In this region of the upper Negro, as well as in São Gabriel de Cachóeira, vampire bats seem to be prolific and they are no better now than in the days of Richard Spruce".*[23]

Through the years, Mee did indeed endure enormous privations and dangers. However, in spite of all this, an *"indomitable force took her always on and on to learn more about the forest flowers and immortalize them with her brush".*[24] Having traveled great distances over long periods of time, she witnessed firsthand the decimation of the Amazon forest as it gave way to unconstrained commercialization.

Fortunately, just as the journals of the earlier explorers captivated the attention of the public in the nineteenth century, so Margaret Mee's diaries and paintings have caught the interest of the public today. Before her death, she had become an important international spokeswoman for the preservation of the Brazilian rainforest. Professor Schultes aptly described Mee as *"the quiet and unostentatious voice of the wilderness (who) can be credited with one of the loudest voices for conservation"*. (25)

Just as these explorers before her opened up the then largely unknown world of Amazonian botany against unimaginable odds, Margaret Mee battled against the forces that threatened to destroy it. Sir Ghillean Prance calls her *"one of the great Amazon explorers of this century"*. (26) Professor Schultes, in comparing Mee's career to that of Spruce, sums it up as follows; *"Their very different material contributions, her life-like paintings, his dried herbarium material of hundreds of species new to science, have given a powerful impetus to the growing outcry against the uncontrolled devastation of the largest rain forest left on the globe"*. (27) Truly, Margaret Mee embodies the spirit of the great explorers who have gone before and holds a rightful place in the distinguished company of Humboldt, Martius, Wallace, Bates and Spruce.

Above: Herbarium specimen of the lovely, night-booming waterlily, *Nymphaea rudgeana*, discovered at Óbidos, on the Rio Amazonas, by Richard Spruce

Below: In 1980, Margaret Mee painted *Nymphaea rudgeana*, originally discovered by Richard Spruce in 1849

NOTES

(1)   M. Mee, Flowers of the Amazon, Rio de Janeiro, 1980.

(2)   H. W. Bates, The Naturalist on the River Amazons, London, 1863, vol.1, iii.

(3)   R. E. Schultes, "Richard Spruce, the Man," Richard Spruce (1817-1893): Botanist and Explorer, London, 1996, 22.

(4)   W. Dean, Brazil and the Struggle for Rubber: A Study in Environmental History, London, 1987.

(5)   R. E. Schultes, "Richard Spruce Still Lives", The Northern Gardener (1953), 7, 22. [Also issued as repaginated reprint, pp. 1-27.]

(6)   J. Ewan, "Tracking Richard Spruce's legacy from George Bentham to Edward Whymper," Richard Spruce (1817-1893): Botanist and Explorer, London, 1996, 42.

(7)   L. B. Smith and M. Mee, The Bromeliads, South Brunswick, N. J., 1969.

(8)   M. Mee, Margaret Mee - In Search of Flowers of the Amazon Forests (ed. T. Morrison), Woodbridge, 1988, 12.

(9)   Ibid., 11.

(10)   R. Spruce, Notes of a Botanist on the Amazon and Andes, (ed. A. R. Wallace), London, 1908, vol. 1, 276.

(11)   Ibid., vol. 1, 266.

(12)   Ibid., vol. 1, 291.

(13)   Ibid., vol. 1, 354.

(14)   Mee, op. cit. (8), 118.

(15)   Ibid., 83.

(16)   Ibid., 85.

(17)   Spruce, op. cit. (10), vol. 2, 208-209.

(18)   Ibid., vol. 1, 275.

(19)   Mee, op. cit. (8), 136.

(20)   Ibid., 125.

(21)   Spruce, op. cit. (10), vol. 1, 279.

(22)   Ibid., vol. 1, 300.

(23)   Mee, op. cit. (8), 122.

(24)   Jardim, M. (ed.). Margaret Mee: Life and Legacy, Rio de Janiero, 1992.

(25)   Mee, op. cit. (8), 12.

(26)   S. Mayo, Margaret Mee's Amazon, London, 1988.

(27)   Mee, op. cit. (8), 12.

Margaret Mee

RETURN TO THE
AMAZON

ROYAL
BOTANIC
GARDENS
KEW

ROYAL   BOTANIC   GARDENS   KEW

Gustavia pulchra, 1979 (family Lecythidaceae)
Pencil and gouache on paper. 661 x 483 mm.
Collection: Library, Royal Botanic Gardens, Kew.

Gustavia pulchra, a striking species restricted to the upper and middle Rio Negro as well as nearby regions of Venezuela, occurs in the understory of periodically flooded lowland forests. It produces spectacular snow-white flowers up to 12.5 cm. across. Born below the leaves, the blooms sprout directly from the branches, a characteristic trait known as cauliflory, common among rainforest trees. G. *pulchra,* normally eight to ten meters, can reach a height of 18 meters. Like numerous other Amazonian species, it was first discovered by the indefatigable 19th century English explorer, Richard Spruce, during his extraordinary journeys throughout Amazonia and the Andes between 1849 and 1864.

During her many years of exploration, Margaret Mee observed the steadily growing threats to the Amazonian forests. Compelled by the need to convey a conservation message through her work, she began to draw the plants in their forest background in a number of her paintings. From the *Leopoldinia palm* in the background, to the humming bird alighting on the inflorescence of the *Gustavia* in the foreground, Margaret seeks to impress on the observer the interdependency of forest species and the importance of preserving their natural habitats.

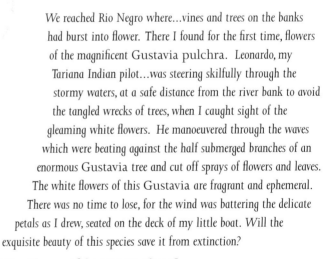

We reached Rio Negro where...vines and trees on the banks had burst into flower. There I found for the first time, flowers of the magnificent Gustavia pulchra. Leonardo, my Tariana Indian pilot...was steering skilfully through the stormy waters, at a safe distance from the river bank to avoid the tangled wrecks of trees, when I caught sight of the gleaming white flowers. He manoeuvered through the waves which were beating against the half submerged branches of an enormous Gustavia tree and cut off sprays of flowers and leaves. The white flowers of this Gustavia are fragrant and ephemeral. There was no time to lose, for the wind was battering the delicate petals as I drew, seated on the deck of my little boat. Will the exquisite beauty of this species save it from extinction?
[M. Mee, **Flowers of the Amazon,** Plate 1]

Gustavia pulchra, Margaret Mee field sketch

Gustavia pulchra
Amazonas

Margaret Mee

Couroupita subsessilis, 1984 (family Lecythidaceae)
Pencil and gouache on paper. 661 x 483 mm.
Collection: Library, Royal Botanic Gardens, Kew.

Flowering throughout the year, *Couroupita subsessilis* displays cauliflory in a sensational manner, particularly amongst the older trees whose trunks and large branches become heavy with fleshy flowers and massive fruit. *C. subsessilis* is widely distributed in the várzea (seasonally flooded) forests along the primary white water rivers of western and central Amazonia, from Iquitos to Manaus and also further east in the areas near Santarém.

Known as the cannonball tree genus, it is aptly named for its cylindrical fruits which fall to the ground when mature. The native people along the Amazon use the foul-smelling pulp as fodder for pigs and chickens. Wild pigs are also thought to feed on the pulp, thus helping to disperse the seeds enveloped within the indehiscent fruits.

The hired boat was a trifle inadequate, as we discovered on our way...Nevertheless, every moment of the journey was fascinating. The Paraná Yamundá is not to be recommended for spectacular Amazon scenery, and cattle are mainly responsible for the somewhat shabby landscape...Trees are almost confined to a dozen or so species: Couroupita - cannonball tree, sapucaia - a lecythid whose seeds can be eaten, Ficus of the Moraceae family and jauarí palms being preponderant...Lois, the assistant botanist, and I wandered over pathless fields and there sighted Clusia flowers on a large bush, but the bush was owned by a snake and we decided not to dispute his territorial rights.

[M. Mee (edited T. Morrison), **Margaret Mee: In Search of Flowers of the Amazon Forests,** Journey Fourteen]

Symphonia globulifera, 1985 (family Clusiaceae)
Pencil and gouache on paper. 661 x 483 mm.
Collection: Library, Royal Botanic Gardens, Kew.

The genus *Symphonia* is distributed in both tropical Africa and tropical America. However, *Symphonia globulifera* is the only species found in the Americas, where it is widespread in many types of forest. A medium-sized to large tree, it can reach a height of approximately 35 meters. The bright yellow sap located in its tissues, easily obtained when branches or bark are cut, is utilized medicinally by the Amazonian Indians in a variety of ways. The plant in the painting comes from the Paraná Yamundá, a tributary of the Rio Trombetas.

Faro is one of the most charming towns I have visited in Amazonia and Pará...We set off early in the morning as the days were sunny and warm, and soon reached a beautiful shore...Landing from time to time on the laterite rocks of the shore I was entranced by the vegetation...The most spectacular of all the trees was a tall guttiferae (Symphonia globulifera), with a trunk clear of branches up to the crown. Seeking light, the flowers grew in brilliant scarlet-cerise clusters above the spreading branches. I remembered having seen one or two groups of these impressive trees as I sailed up the Nhamundá. That time they had been far out of reach, but here I found a tree which had been felled and lay on the ground, so I gathered some of the rare flowers. I could have spent many days on this enchanted lake with its wealth of plants; nevertheless as the journey proceeded, new delights appeared.

[M. Mee (edited T. Morrison), **Margaret Mee: In Search of Flowers of the Amazon Forests,** Journey Fourteen]

Symphonia globulifera, Margaret Mee field sketch

Margaret Mee

Unknown plant, 1972
Pencil and gouache on paper. 661 x 483 mm.
Collection: Library, Royal Botanic Gardens, Kew.

Margaret Mee collected this plant along the Rio Urubaxi in Amazonas. The red, bell-shaped fruits of the small tree, which grows to a height of about four to five meters, contain seeds suspended within the receptacle that change over time from green to blue-black. The initial attempt to identify this plant placed it in the *Ochnaceae* family, but the shape of the calyx seems to suggest otherwise and botanists are likely to remain mystified until the species is recollected in flower.

Moving up Rio Jurubaxi I caught sight of a small tree which stood deep in the water, glowing with cerise coloured fruit, or were they flowers? On closer inspection I realised that they were red calices like little sunshades, sheltering black and green fruit. So we stopped, while I quickly painted them. As a result that night we were late finding shelter for the men, but eventually discovered a deserted hut at the top of a steep bank, almost out of sight from my canoe which was moored amongst a group of trees out in the river. I slept soundly and in the morning was rather surprised at the wan appearance of Leonardo and João. They had scarcely slept, it appeared, for in the igapó just across the narrow river they heard a prowling onça (jaguar). I asked why they had not warned me, and with Indian logic, Leonardo replied that he did not know whether the jaguar would choose the hut or the boat!

[M. Mee, **Flowers of the Amazon,** Plate 4]

Margaret Mee

Ochna
Amazonas, Rio Guaribasi, June, 1972

Heterostemon mimosoides, 1978 (family Leguminosae)
Pencil and gouache on paper. 661 x 483 mm.
Collection: Library, Royal Botanic Gardens, Kew.

Heterostemon is a small genus of less than ten species restricted in its distribution to northwest Brazil and the bordering areas of Colombia and Venezuela. Although it was first described as early as 1818, it is poorly known with the exception of the species Heterostemon mimosoides.

With its abundant, orchidlike flowers and splendid foliage, Heterostemon mimosoides is one of the most lovely of all American leguminous plants. It is a low growing shrub or small tree ranging from two to ten meters tall, commonly found in the igapó and várzea forests (permanent and seasonal swamp forests) of the Uaupés and Rio Negro rivers, particularly in the vicinity of Ega and Manaus. Margaret's plant was collected from the Rio Cuieiras, a left bank tributary of the Rio Negro near Manaus.

My ... encounter with this beautiful tree, with its amethyst flowers and deep green leaves that resemble those of Mimosa, was on the Rio Cuieiras, a tributary of the great Rio Negro. There, seated in my boat, I was successful in capturing the colour and form before the fragile flowers drooped and faded. Heterostemon mimosoides is the tree of which Richard Spruce wrote more than a century ago in his book **(Notes of a Botanist on the Amazon and Andes)** - "...a leguminous tree which was in flower all the way up the river and formed a great ornament to its banks." And later, Adolpho Ducke, the great Brazilian botanist, described it as "probably the most beautiful of all Brazilian Leguminosae".

[M. Mee, **Flowers of the Amazon,** Plate 2]

Gustavia augusta, 1985 (family Lecythidaceae)
Pencil and gouache on paper. 730 x 507 mm.
Collection: Library, Royal Botanic Gardens, Kew.

In 1775, the genus *Gustavia* was founded on the type species, *Gustavia augusta,* by the Swedish botanist, Carl Linnaeus, whose work, *Species Plantarum* (1753), established the universal scientific language for the formal naming and describing of plants - the binomial system of nomenclature. Linnaeus dedicated the new genus, which now includes about forty-one species, to Gustavus III (1746-92), King of Sweden, who supported him in his botanical quests.

Gustavia augusta, a medium-sized tree that reaches a height of about 20 meters, can be found along river margins and other habitats with periodically flooded soil. It is widely distributed throughout the Guianas, Surinam, Venezuela, Peru, and Brazil. In a complex, aesthetically pleasing arrangement, Margaret has depicted *Gustavia augusta* within its natural habitat of epiphytic aroids, orchids, and bromeliads, together with the symmetry of the hanging nests of the oropendula bird, the graceful arches of the *Mauritia* palm, and the elegance of the white egret.

As we got further upstream the rivers became more and more fascinating. Jará palms grew in humid places along the banks, sometimes almost covered by the high water, their fibrous stems making wonderful homes for dozens of epiphytes. Groups of perfumed orchids, including Galeandra devoniana, bloomed profusely...Trees of Gustavia augusta, with large pink and white flowers, were frequent and I felt I should have stopped, collected and sketched. But that had to wait...

[M. Mee (edited T. Morrison), **Margaret Mee: In Search of Flowers of the Amazon Forests,** Journey Four]

Gustavia augusta, Margaret Mee field sketches

Gustavia augusta
Amazonas Feb 1988

Margaret Mee

Memora schomburgkii, 1984 (family Bignoniaceae)
Pencil and gouache on paper. 661 x 483 mm.
Collection: Library, Royal Botanic Gardens, Kew.

The Bignoniaceae is a predominantly woody family that includes numerous large trees and many striking lianas, woody climbing plants that form a characteristic and important element in tropical rainforests. The 19th century English explorer, Richard Spruce, described them memorably with his characteristic dry wit:

"there is scarcely any family of plants which does not include some members who get up in the world by scrambling upon their more robust and self-standing neighbours . Where two or more of these vagabonds come into collision in mid-air, and find nothing else to twine upon, they twine around each other as closely as the strands of a cable, and the stronger of them generally ends by squeezing the life out of the weaker".

Memora schomburgkii is found in the Guianas and Amazonia. The handsome trumpet-shaped flowers are characteristic of this plant, and their leaves tend to be subdivided pinnately, like those of an ash tree. The long pendulous pods that form its fruit initially appear very similar to those of legumes. Margaret collected this plant in Oriximiná, Pará, near the mouth of the Rio Trombetas, one of the largest northern tributaries in lower Amazonia.

I travelled overland along the new road…to Óbidos, an old town at the narrowest point of the lower river. The journey was a bitter disappointment, as I had read the descriptions of the countryside by nineteenth century travellers, among them Henry Bates who wrote that the hills and lowlands there were covered with forest. I will write while I am still in a state of visual shock on the 'road'…the landscape (what is left of it), is a sad stretch of capoeira [wasteland], and where once virgin forest existed, there is now a blackened sea of giant skeletons. Embaúbas are struggling to regenerate the almost exterminated jungle.

In spite of the destruction and fencing in of the land, I have found a survivor, a marvellous vine, Memora schomburgkii…

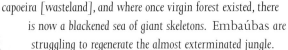

[M. Mee (edited T. Morrison), **Margaret Mee: In Search of Flowers of the Amazon Forests,** Journey Thirteen]

Memora schomburgkii, Margaret Mee field sketch

Margaret Mee

Psittacanthus cinctus, 1982 (family Loranthaceae)
Pencil and gouache on paper. 730 x 507 mm.
Collection: Library, Royal Botanic Gardens, Kew.

Psittacanthus cinctus belongs to the largest family of mistletoes, Loranthaceae, comprising
approximately 65 genera and 900 species. As woody plants, mistletoes develop a parasitic
attachment to their host tree. However, they are not totally reliant on their hosts as they are
photosynthetic and thereby able to synthesize sugars using sunlight. The flowers of many of these
plants are especially showy, attracting the attention of birds and insects for pollination.

Margaret Mee's painting accurately depicts the bulging upturned tips of the flowers,
characteristic of this species. Its range extends along the Rio Negro from Manaus in Brazil to
the Amazonian region of Venezuela. Richard Spruce is known to have collected this plant in
1851, growing on lecythid trees (brazil nut family) near Manaus, known at that time as Barra
do Rio Negro.

Loranthaceae
Rio Negro, Amazonas
May 1982

Margaret Mee

Phryganocydia corymbosa, 1985 (family Bignoniaceae)
Pencil and gouache on paper. 661 x 483 mm.
Collection: Library, Royal Botanic Gardens, Kew.

Phryganocydia corymbosa, a widespread tropical American liana, blooms throughout the year producing fragrant flowers which are typically rose, lilac or magenta in color. In addition, white-flowered plants may also be found, but only in select areas. As the most common species of the Bignoniaceae family in the Canal Zone and eastern Panama, its range extends southward to include Brazil. Margaret collected this plant near the mouth of the Rio Trombetas, not far from Santarém, the area where Spruce collected it one hundred and thirty years previously.

A visiting botanist, Klaus Kubitski, invited me to accompany him and his assistant, Lais Sonkin, on a journey west along the Paraná Yamundá to Lago Faro where he planned to collect specimens from trees in flower. I accepted this kind invitation with alacrity...In spite of the rather sterile surroundings I collected a lovely white bignone, the trumpet vine Phryganocydia corymbosa, which I sketched on board, working far into the night.

[M. Mee (edited T. Morrison), **Margaret Mee: In Search of Flowers of the Amazon Forests,** Journey Fourteen]

Phryganocydia corymbosa, Margaret Mee field sketch

Margaret Mee
September, 1964

Phryganocydia corymbosa (Vent.) Bur.
Rio Yamunda, Pará

Clusia grandifolia, 1983 (family Clusiaceae)
Pencil and gouache on paper. 730 x 507 mm.
Collection: Library, Royal Botanic Gardens, Kew.

In the Amazon region, the common name for the genus *Clusia* is 'Rosa da Mata' (Rose of the Forest). Several species are cultivated for their striking ornamental flowers and foliage, yet they have a more sinister side. As members of the well-known group of rain-forest plants commonly known as stranglers, the *Clusia* seedlings and juveniles begin life as epiphytes on a host tree. After some time their aerial roots reach the ground, and thereafter join laterally. Despite the name of strangler, the roots themselves do not actually kill the enclosed host tree. Rather the *Clusia* overtops and shades outs its host as it grows.

Clusia grandifolia was first discovered by the 19th century Yorkshire botanist, Richard Spruce, who found it in 1852 on the Rio Uaupés, a tributary of the Rio Negro in *igapó* (flooded) forest. It has also been collected on occasion from neighboring regions of Venezuela.

Today I made colour sketches of a beautiful clusia which I could just reach on the bank; it was no easy matter, seated in the boat which was rolling in the swell of the river. This is the first time I have seen a perfect specimen of this species, Clusia grandiflora, *which is a coral colour inside and white outside, looking like a precious piece of porcelain.*

[M. Mee (edited T. Morrison), **Margaret Mee: In Search of Flowers of the Amazon Forests,** Journey Five]

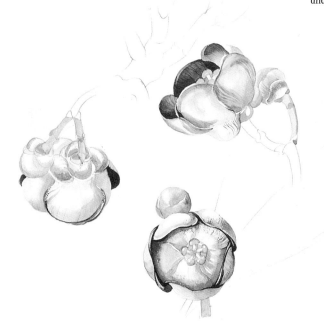

Clusia grandifolia, Margaret Mee field sketch

Clusia nemorosa, 1973 (family Clusiaceae)
Pencil and gouache on paper. 661 x 483 mm.
Collection: Library, Royal Botanic Gardens, Kew.

The geographical distribution of the small tree *Clusia nemorosa* is interesting in that it is one of a large group of species to be found both in Amazonia and eastern Brazil, but not in the seasonally dry region in between. Its habitat includes the Guianas, the narrow natural channels of the Upper Rio Negro and the edge of rivers such as the Xingu, where it is more widespread and better known than *Clusia grandifolia*. In eastern Brazil, it is known to occur along the coastal forest region known as the 'Mata Atlântica'.

From the Rio Joarí we had a magnificent view of the Serra do Araçá and Pico Rondon. The scenery was superb...I was reminded of a visit I had made in June to a Tushaua (Chief) on Rio Madeira, a Cacique without a tribe, who had welcomed me with a grand gesture, 'Welcome to our Domain!' And later in my journey I met the same independent spirit in another Tushaua whose tribe had moved far into the forest where he would be following them. But before leaving, feeling that I was a guest in his domain, he led me into the forest to collect plants, and where, as we stepped out of the canoe on to the wet rocks, I found this lovely Clusia nemorosa.

[M. Mee, **Flowers of the Amazon,** Plate 3]

Clusia nemorosa G.F.W.Meyer
Amazonas, Rio Araca

Margaret Mee

Clusia sp. (possibly **C. grandiflora**), 1987 (family Clusiaceae)
Pencil and gouache on paper. 661 x 483 mm.
Collection: Library, Royal Botanic Gardens, Kew.

The Clusiaceae family includes trees, shrubs, or lianas which are known for their viscous sap, with several species yielding resins and valuable timber. The largest genus, *Clusia,* is found solely in tropical America.

Although this plant, which Margaret collected along the upper Rio Negro, has not yet been positively identified, it is thought to be *Clusia grandiflora.* The habitat of this species, with a somewhat restricted range, also includes eastern Amazonia, and has been found in Surinam, Guyana, and the Brazilian state of Pará in the region of Belém.

In the early hours of the morning the river's face was covered with a dense white mist. As the sky began to get a first flush of rose and gold, the mists lifted like a gossamer curtain, and the chill humidity gave way to the burning heat of day. We passed by the Serra of Bela Vista, at dawn...I saw that we were passing the most wonderful, flowered-filled forests. There was an abundance of clusias with white blossoms (Clusia grandiflora?)...After the little village of NaNa there appeared on the riverbanks, framed by the dark trees, what seemed to be large groups of sculpture. As we drew nearer, I saw that they were great stones, weathered into strange forms by the elements.

[Excerpt from Margaret Mee's Journals].

Clusia sp (possibly *C. grandiflora*), Margaret Mee field sketch

Margaret Ellis
November 1974

Heliconia unnamed species, 1981 (family Heliconiaceae)
Pencil and gouache on paper. 661 x 483 mm.
Collection: Library, Royal Botanic Gardens, Kew.

Native to Central and South America and a number of South Pacific islands, heliconias are robust, fast-growing, forest-floor herbs. Like the bananas to which they are related, they may reach vast sizes, but their elegant flowering shoots give them a characteristic beauty all their own. The flowers are small and borne within the large, often vividly-colored bracts (modified leaves), whose shapes often resemble birds in flight. Although the inflorescences are pendent in many species, they may be erect in others. These remarkable plants rely on their distinct and brilliantly-colored inflorescences to serve as strong visual signals for attraction, the result of adaptation to pollination by birds.

Although numerous new species of *Heliconia* have been discovered in the last two decades, these plants have been poorly known until quite recently. As a result, many have yet to be named, such as the plant in this painting.

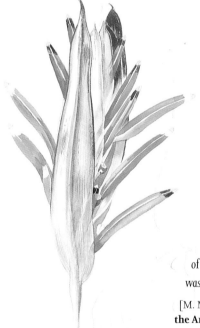

Four Tucano Indian girls from the mission borrowed a canoe and took me with them to collect plants, paddling past the rapids and landing in a caatinga (forest of short spindly trees). *As I wandered through this strange dry forest...I chanced upon a primitive shelter. Hesitantly I approached and found two Indians, a wrinkled old Maké and a young Dinian boy making curare arrow poison in an earthen pot. They were shy and obviously found it difficult to communicate, but did not seem to mind me watching the intricate process. I could not help thinking it was quite remarkable that generations ago the forest people had discovered a blend of plant extracts which could kill by relaxing the muscles. We came out of the caatinga into a dark jungle of giant trees where scarlet heliconias grew shoulder high and the ground was carpeted with moss and selaginellas.*

[M. Mee (edited T. Morrison), **Margaret Mee: In Search of Flowers of the Amazon Forests,** Journey Three]

Heliconia unnamed species, Margaret Mee field sketch

Heliconia chartacea, 1975 (family Heliconiaceae)
Pencil and gouache on paper. 661 x 483 mm.
Collection: Library, Royal Botanic Gardens, Kew.

Described as recently as 1972, *Heliconia chartacea* occurs in western Amazonia. It is conspicuous in the understorey of the forest because of the cinnamon red bracts enclosing the much smaller flowers. Attracted by the intense red color, hummingbirds are commonly seen hovering over these plants.

Margaret's painting is of a cultivated plant from the gardens of the late Roberto Burle Marx, Brazil's most celebrated landscape architect and artist. Marx had an outstanding collection of the genus, and frequently used many different species of *Heliconia* in his designs for tropical gardens. He was a great friend of Margaret's and on occasion would journey with her to collect rare plants. In the preface to her diaries, **Margaret Mee: In Search of Flowers of the Amazon Forests** (Nonesuch Expeditions, 1988), Marx professed his fascination with the Heliconia genus. "In hollows near the rivers the heliconias develop a theme of extraordinary richness and variety...I see them as sculpture, as forms projected in space, shapes enriched by the tension between flowers and leaves."

The beautiful country house and estate of the great landscapist and artist Roberto Burle Marx, are well known to Cariocas and visitors from all over Brazil, as well as tourists from many parts of the world. Over the years Roberto Burle Marx has collected plants from every corner of Brazil and from other South American countries...Many of the plants in this collection have been rescued from areas where Nature has been completely obliterated; others come from regions threatened with destruction; but all are being cultivated with love and infinite care, so that one day when man comes to his senses, the progeny can be returned to the original ambient...It was in the peace of this garden, amongst a world of flowers and birds, that I painted the Heliconia chartacea.

[M. Mee, **Flowers of the Amazon,** Plate 22]

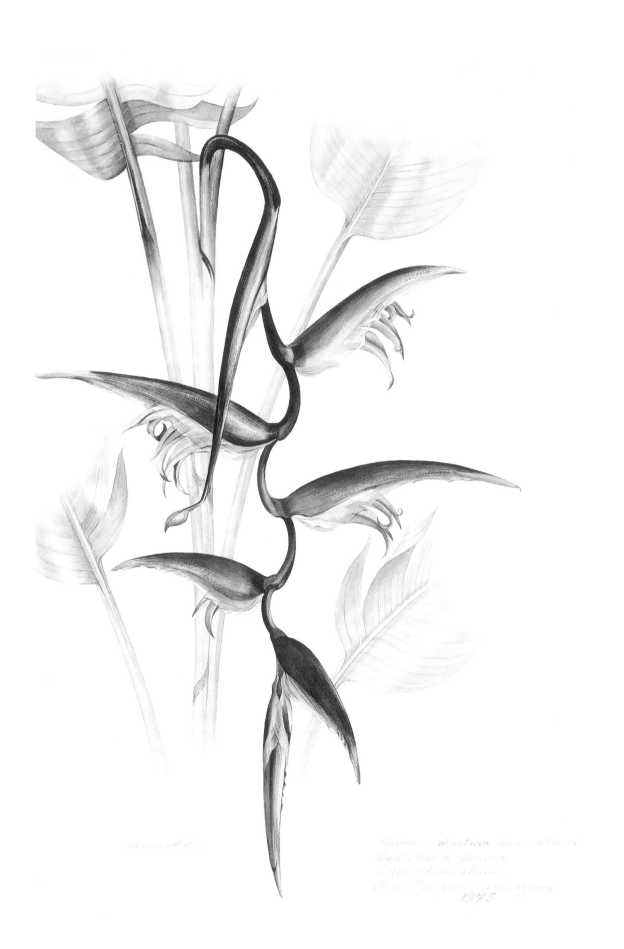

Heliconia chartacea var. ...
... ...
... ...
... ...
1975

Margaret Mee

Heliconia unnamed species, undated (family Heliconiaceae)
Pencil and gouache on paper. 661 x 483 mm.
Collection: Library, Royal Botanic Gardens, Kew.

Since the founding of the Heliconia Society International in 1985, heliconias have become increasingly popular as landscaping plants throughout the tropics and subtropics. In regions where they cannot be grown in outdoor gardens, they are grown as potted plants and cut flowers.

Margaret collected this plant along the Rio Uaupés, a tributary of the Rio Negro. The drawing presents a fine and finished example of her ability to combine botanical accuracy with superb compositional arrangement. The delicate wash of foliage conveys a knowing understanding of the leaves even as they fade off into the distance. The inflorescence is captivating in its subtle coloration and striking precision of curves and angles. As it has yet to be described, this species of *Heliconia* remains unnamed.

Heliconia uaupensis E.M.
Amazonas, Rio Uaupés

Margaret Mee

Nymphaea rudgeana, 1978 (family Nymphaeaceae)
Pencil and gouache on paper. 661 x 483 mm.
Collection: Library, Royal Botanic Gardens, Kew.

Rarely seen in cultivation, this tropical night-blooming waterlily is a smaller relative of the well-known *Victoria amazonica*, the giant Amazonian waterlily that has, since the last century, remained a coveted show plant of botanic gardens worldwide. Distributed throughout the West Indies and the Amazonian regions of Brazil and its neighboring countries, *Nymphaea rudgeana* often makes its home in the slow flowing waters of lowland coastal habitats.

The intrepid English explorer and botanist, Richard Spruce, first discovered this species in 1849 at Óbidos, on the Rio Amazonas near Santarém. Its greenish-yellow flowers, eight to nine centimeters in diameter, reportedly open at dusk for two or three successive nights, emitting a pleasing lemon scent that attracts its pollinator, a scarab beetle. Among the new hybrid waterlilies are several with *rudgeana* characteristics.

Does this beautiful lake where I found Nymphaea rudgeana in flower still exist? They were putting the surrounding primary forest to axe and fire. Enormous trees, many of which may have existed at the time when the great botanist Von Martius was exploring the Amazon, had been wantonly felled to make a road from the small village to nowhere, passing through the finest virgin forest I have ever seen...The lake verged on land which had been completely transformed from the original exuberant forest to a miserable capoeira...Starred by white Nymphaeas, and overshadowed by Buriti palms which arose in their midst, this breathless lake gleamed. Myriads of climbing plants had woven themselves into the fibrous stems of the Buritis and hung in motionless cascades over the water. Butterflies and dragonflies skimmed the mirror surface of the lake giving movement and life to this enchanted place. I hope that the enormous Black Onça of Indian legends dwells at the bottom of the lake to protect it from the ravages of man.

[M. Mee, **Flowers of the Amazon,** Plate 23]

margaret mee

Philodendron arcuatum, 1977 (family Araceae)
Pencil and gouache on paper. 661 x 483 mm.
Collection: Library, Royal Botanic Gardens, Kew.

A member of the Araceae family, which includes climbers, epiphytes and hemiepiphytes, *Philodendron arcuatum* is a climbing epiphyte whose stems are coated with a thick layer of rusty-brown, coarse hairs, a peculiar characteristic also exhibited in other species. Although it is not well known, *P. arcuatum* is quite widespread throughout western Amazonia, Bolivia, and the Guianas. Margaret's painting of this species is the only color illustration known.

Igarapé das Lajes, 130 km, distant from Manaus, flows beside a unique and beautiful rock formation, surrounded by forest...About a year ago, this ensemble formed a natural rock-garden...Then a family of posseiros moved in and reduced most of this beauty to ashes...With heavy hearts my companion and I made our way towards the more secluded forest where Nature still reigns supreme, stopping beside a small lake fringed by the mottled leaves of aroids imitating the light and shade of the woodlands...To my delight, the aroid for which I was searching in the destroyed rock-garden existed here clinging to many of the slender trees beside the igarapé. We crossed the limpid stream, and in the all-pervading beauty of our surroundings momentarily forgot the devastation that man is wreaking wherever he sets foot.

[M. Mee, **Flowers of the Amazon,** Plate 13]

Philodendron arcuatum, Margaret Mee field sketches

Urospatha sagittifolia, 1976 (family Araceae)
Pencil and gouache on paper. 661 x 483 mm.
Collection: Library, Royal Botanic Gardens, Kew.

Urospatha sagittifolia, a striking wetland plant, is outstanding for its elongated, corkscrew-tipped inflorescences and large triangular leaves. Several species of the related genus, Cyrtosperma, from south-east Asia, also produce curiously twisted floral spathes, pointing to ancient contacts between the plants of the Old and New Worlds.

With a widespread distribution throughout the Guianas, most of Amazonia, and reaching as far east as Bahia, this species grows in large stands on marshy ground along river banks.

Many years ago I voyaged on the beautiful Rio Uaupés and wandered around São Gabriel da Cachóeira...A superb view of the Serra de Curicuriari dominated the distance beyond the gleaming Rio Uaupés. This was the serra which Richard Spruce had climbed and explored more than a hundred years ago. There he discovered many new species of plants and trees, some of which bear his name...Nature was exuberant in São Gabriel. In the swamps beside the path, a strange aroid thrust long stems with arrow shaped leaves, and the olive green flower spathes twisted in long spirals. Alone, I was unable to reach these plants, but guarded them closely in my memory as a future painting... Eventually a botanist brought this plant to me, and I was able to trace the subtle lines and follow the dark colours of Urospatha sagittifolia in the seclusion of my terrace...

[M. Mee, **Flowers of the Amazon,** Plate 12]

Streptocalyx poeppigii, 1985 (family Bromeliaceae)
Pencil and gouache on paper. 730 x 507 mm.
Collection: Library, Royal Botanic Gardens, Kew.

Streptocalyx poeppigii belongs to the bromeliad or pineapple family, a group of over two thousand species that are mainly epiphytes - plants that grow on other plants without feeding on them. The genus *Streptocalyx,* comprising 14 species of terrestrial (growing in the ground) or epiphytic bromeliads, is distributed throughout Brazil, Ecuador, Colombia, and eastern Peru. It was named by the notable Austrian botanist, Johann Georg Beer, who published the first monograph devoted to bromeliads, *Die Familie der Bromeliaceen,* in 1857.

Streptocalyx poeppigii, distributed widely throughout Colombia to Amazonian Brazil and Bolivia, was collected by and named for the distinguished German botanist and explorer, Eduard Poeppig (1798-1868), who made a significant early expedition to the Amazonian area of both Peru and Brazil. This bromeliad grows as an epiphyte in the rain forest but occasionally may be seen growing terrestrially, adapting to altitudes ranging from 25-1200 meters. Its robust inflorescence, with rose-purple flowers, is replaced by pink and white berries which gradually turn purple in color and remain for months.

Streptocalyx longifolius, 1982 (family Bromeliaceae)
Pencil and gouache on paper. 730 x 507 mm.
Collection: Library, Royal Botanic Gardens, Kew.

Streptocalyx longifolius, native to the rainforests from Brazil to north-east Peru, is a typical ant-inhabited bromeliad, with thousands of biting ants living in its large leaf sheaths, making it very difficult to collect. The French botanist, Joseph Martin, discovered *Streptocalyx longifolius* in French Guiana in the early 1800's. Unfortunately for him, his prized collections ended up in the hands of the British when the ship carrying it back to France was seized by English privateers in 1803.

Growing up to 92 cm. in height, *S. longifolius* is a dense rosette of spiny light-green leaves with a striking, pallid pink inflorescence (cluster of flowers) borne on a short scape. These epiphytic plants thrive in the hot, humid conditions of the rainforests, occurring from Brazil to north-east Peru. Margaret collected this beautiful bromeliad along the Rio Negro on her fifth journey.

Next morning we returned to the boat accompanied by Felipe and Domingo who came to help us cross the cachóeiras (rapids). Truly we needed their help for the boat had to be lifted over the rocks and dragged through the raging torrent. It took over an hour to pass the first fall with much sweating and straining...The only way up was among rocks near the bank, and the two Indians used long poles to lever the hull across the obstruction which took until midday to pass. Finally we were over the rapids and, completely exhausted, settled on a group of big stones beside calmer water...It was a splendid place for plant collecting and there I found Streptocalyx longifolius - a bromeliad with tremendously long leaves...

[M. Mee (edited T. Morrison), **Margaret Mee: In Search of Flowers of the Amazon Forests,** Journey Five]

Streptocalyx longifolius, Margaret Mee field sketch

Margaret Mee   Streptocalyx longifolia
                                Amazonas, Rio Negro
                                May, 1972

Vriesea heliconioides, 1973 (family Bromeliaceae)
Pencil and gouache on paper. 661 x 483 mm.
Collection: Library, Royal Botanic Gardens, Kew.

The genus *Vriesea*, named after the Dutch botanist, W. H. de Vries (1807-1862), was established by the British taxonomist John Lindley in 1843, and contains more than 225 species, with new ones constantly being discovered. These plants are distributed over a large area from Mexico, Central America, and the West Indies to Peru, Bolivia, Argentina and Brazil. Seeking dappled light combined with good air circulation, vrieseas grow epiphytically on tree branches in the rainforest at altitudes between 100 and 950 meters, forming vase-shaped rosettes with their broad leaves. Their highly colored floral bracts remain vivid for weeks.

This painting of a plant from the Rio Demini, Amazonas depicts the spectacular *Vriesia heliconioides* in bloom, with its brilliant red flower spike edged with chartreuse and surrounded by smooth green leaves suffused with red. This species was first discovered in 1801 by the indefatigable explorers Alexander von Humboldt and his assistant Aimé Bonpland, and is distributed throughout southern Mexico to Bolivia and western Brazil.

Vriesia heliconioides, Margaret Mee field sketch

Aechmea tillandsioides, 1976 (family Bromeliaceae)
Pencil and gouache on paper. 661 x 483 mm.
Collection: Library, Royal Botanic Gardens, Kew.

The genus *Aechmea*, comprising almost 200 species, was named in 1794 by the Spanish naturalists and explorers Hipolito Ruiz and Sebastian José Pavón. Aechmeas are well known for their vividly colored foliage and long lasting, prominent flower crowns. Attracted by the nectar of the flowers, hummingbirds are known to pollinate many species of *Aechmea*. Although they are native to central Mexico south to Argentina, the main area of distribution for these plants is Brazil, where they grow epiphytically on trees in tropical cloud and rainforests and rarely on the ground. They have also been found in dry regions.

Aechmea tillandsioides, reaching a height of 50 cm. when in flower, forms an upright funnel-shaped rosette with leathery, grayish-green leaves edged with spines, each leaf being pointed at its tip. Its small yellow flower petals are followed by long-lasting, ornamental berries which are first white in color, then blue. This species was discovered on the Rio Japurá in Colombia in 1820 by the distinguished German botanist, Karl von Martius (1794-1868). His monumental, fifteen volume work on Brazilian flora, *Flora Brasiliensis* was completed 38 years following his death by a team of international botanists.

The River Papagaio, true to its name, was swarming with parrots of all kinds...Once, Paulo the mateiro, collecting an Aechmea tillandsioides in a very tall tree, called down that he could see a Parrot's nest below, with two fledglings. The parent birds circled around, screaming frantically, and I entreated him to come down immediately and to leave them in peace...We embarked in the canoe and paddled through the silent igapó until the lowering sky threatened a violent storm...Just as we reached our boat the storm broke with thundering fury, the wind driving sheets of rain towards us with hurricane force, obliterating everything around. It was many hours before the storm abated and the waters calmed down, and as darkness was falling we moored in the igapó for the night.
[M. Mee, **Flowers of the Amazon,** Plate 7]

Aechmea polyantha, 1973 (family Bromeliaceae)
Pencil and gouache on paper. 661 x 483 mm.
Collection: Library, Royal Botanic Gardens, Kew.

This species was first discovered by Margaret Mee in 1972, growing as an epiphyte in igapó forest (permanent swamp forest) on the Rio Maraú, near Maués, Amazonas.   A splendid bromeliad, reaching nearly one meter in height, *Aechmea polyantha* forms a remarkable ellipsoid tank with its many leathery leaves, edged with spines. Its coral inflorescence is borne on an erect stalk, 25 cm. long. This rare species is known scientifically only from Margaret Mee's collections.

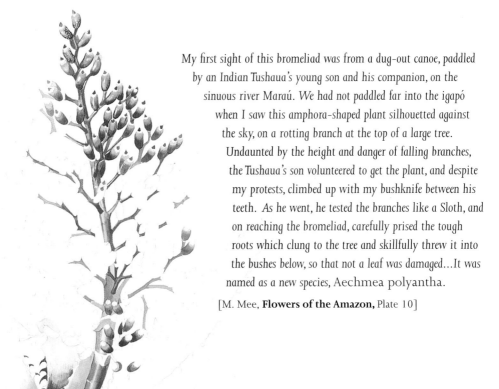

My first sight of this bromeliad was from a dug-out canoe, paddled by an Indian Tushaua's young son and his companion, on the sinuous river Maraú. We had not paddled far into the igapó when I saw this amphora-shaped plant silhouetted against the sky, on a rotting branch at the top of a large tree. Undaunted by the height and danger of falling branches, the Tushaua's son volunteered to get the plant, and despite my protests, climbed up with my bushknife between his teeth. As he went, he tested the branches like a Sloth, and on reaching the bromeliad, carefully prised the tough roots which clung to the tree and skillfully threw it into the bushes below, so that not a leaf was damaged...It was named as a new species, Aechmea polyantha.

[M. Mee, **Flowers of the Amazon,** Plate 10]

Aechmea polyantha Margaret Mee field sketch

Dyckia Polyantha Virgin Islands

Margaret Mee
January 1942

Aechmea meeana, 1978 (family Bromeliaceae)
Pencil and gouache on paper. 661 x 483 mm.
Collection: Library, Royal Botanic Gardens, Kew.

Lyman B. Smith (1904 -), long considered the world's leading authority on Bromeliaceae, named *Aechmea meeana* in honor of its discoverer, Margaret Mee. During Margaret's early years in Brazil, when she was employed at the Instituto de Botânica of São Paulo, she collaborated with Smith on the preparation of a large series of paintings depicting bromeliads of the whole of Brazil. The knowledge she gained from this experience enabled her to discover several previously unknown Amazonian species

Aechmea meeana grows to approximately 70 cm high, with many strap-shaped leaves rising to form a conical vase. Each leathery leaf narrows to a point ending in a woody black spine and is notched along its margins with large, deep-purple spines. The leaves are densely covered with water-absorbing scales, a characteristic common to all bromeliads. This rare bromeliad was collected from the Rio Maraú, near Maués, Amazonas, and remains scientifically known only from Margaret Mee's collections.

When the snows melt on the Andean Mountains a stupendous volume of water flows into the Amazon Basin and, at certain points, rivers rise by as much as 18 meters, resulting in the forests being inundated for hundreds of square miles around. The year of this journey the waters rose exceptionally high on the Rio Maués, making navigation difficult... We had scarcely lost sight of the village, when, in the igapó, through the thick foliage of the tree in which it was growing, gleamed a large bromeliad inflorescence. The branches of pink and purple flowers were protected by an enormous clump of plants armed with formidable thorns. In great excitement I pointed it out to Bento who immediately plunged into the river and climbed into the tree fork, my bushknife between his teeth. He carefully picked out the hairy spiders from the leaf-cups with the point of his knife, then hacked at the woody roots which secured the plants to the tree...To free himself from the tormenting ants he plunged into the river, before returning for another plant of this new species.

[M. Mee, **Flowers of the Amazon,** Plate 8]

Aechmea meeana, Margaret Mee field sketch

Aechmea rodriguesiana, 1977 (family Bromeliaceae)
Pencil and gouache on paper. 661 x 483 mm.
Collection: Library, Royal Botanic Gardens, Kew.

Aechmea rodriguesiana was named in honor of William A. Rodrigues, the notable Brazilian botanist who first discovered it in the area of the Ducke Reserve near Manaus. Margaret collected this plant along the Rio Maraú and depicted it within its rainforest habitat, inserting a twig from a young *Clusia* epiphyte as well as the curious leaves of the aroid, *Philodendron goeldii,* in the background.

Aechmea rodriguesiana grows epiphytically in the region of the lower Amazon and Rio Negro. Its leathery leaves, reaching up to 1.40 meters in length, are edged with thin dark thorns and tipped with red at the apex. The inflorescence rises dramatically above the leaves to a height of 60 cm. on a thick floral scape, covered with scales.

It was early afternoon when we sailed up the tranquil waters of the igarapé do Albino on our way to Rio Amene…There I caught sight of a large bromeliad crowning one of the strangely contorted trees which composed this igapó. The young mateiro plunged into the dark waters and swam across, climbing into the tree with the agility of a monkey. On board I examined the plant. The thorn edged leaves encircled the flower spike like a crown. The flowers were dry and the fruit already forming. As this was a species I had never seen before, I decided to return to the area again in the flowering season…About six months later I returned to Rio Urupadi in my own little boat with my faithful old boatman Severino and the helpful mateiro Bento. After some searching I found Aechmea rodriguesiana again, this time in full flower, the rose pink bracts enclosing pure white florets.
[M. Mee, **Flowers of the Amazon,** Plate 11]

Aechmea rodriguesiana, Margaret Mee field sketch

garet o'lee
July 1977

Aechmea rodriguesiana
Rio Manaus, Amazonas

Aechmea tocantina, 1981 (family Bromeliaceae)
Pencil and gouache on paper. 661 x 483 mm.
Collection: Library, Royal Botanic Gardens, Kew.

Widespread in South America, *Aechmea tocantina* can be found at altitudes ranging between 100 and 700 meters in Venezuela, Guiana, Bolivia and Amazonian Brazil, where it grows epiphytically to a height of one to two meters. It was first discovered by the British botanist Hugh Weddell on the Rio Tocantins, the easternmost major river of southern Amazonia.

Today we went out in the boat...to Lago Surubim, a lake which Paulo said was well stocked with fish...It proved to be all that Paulo claimed, and for one and a half hours we sailed without passing one habitation - just forest and igapó... Dipping along beside the shore and up shady waterways I was able to observe the magnificent plants surrounding the lake. On the outer fringe of forest there was a strange area where dried out shells of trees, riddled by ants and weathered by the beating winds and rains, mingled with young trees bearing luxuriant foliage, many in flower. Epiphytes clustered in their branches - philodendrons with large dark leaves, spiny bromeliads, Aechmea setigera, the very aggressive Aechmea tocantina, armed with black thorns, and giant clumps of Schomburgkia orchids.

[M. Mee (edited T. Morrison), **Margaret Mee: In Search of Flowers of the Amazon Forests,** Journey Twelve]

Aechmea tocantina, Margaret Mee field sketch

Aechmea huebneri, 1977 (family Bromeliaceae)
Pencil and gouache on paper. 661 x 483 mm.
Collection: Library, Royal Botanic Gardens, Kew.

Aechmea huebneri was discovered by and named after the German botanist and collector, G. Hübner, who first encountered it in 1927 along the banks of the Rio Taruma-Mirim, a tributary of the lower Rio Negro in Amazonas. A large plant reaching approximately 1.3 meters high, *A. huebneri* grows terrestrially on open ground and epiphytically in the igapó (permanent swamp forest) to 135 meters altitude. It has an interesting geographical distribution in that it jumps from Amazonia to the eastern coast of Brazil. With its formidable thorns, it is a difficult plant to collect.

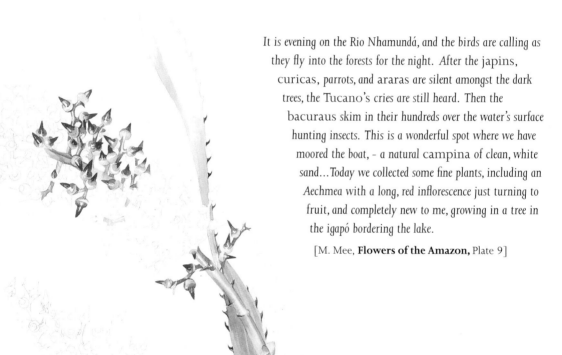

It is evening on the Rio Nhamundá, and the birds are calling as they fly into the forests for the night. After the japins, curicas, parrots, and araras are silent amongst the dark trees, the Tucano's cries are still heard. Then the bacuraus skim in their hundreds over the water's surface hunting insects. This is a wonderful spot where we have moored the boat, - a natural campina of clean, white sand...Today we collected some fine plants, including an Aechmea with a long, red inflorescence just turning to fruit, and completely new to me, growing in a tree in the igapó bordering the lake.

[M. Mee, **Flowers of the Amazon,** Plate 9]

Aechmea huebneri, Margaret Mee field sketch

Neoregelia margaretae, 1979 (family Bromeliaceae)
Pencil and gouache on paper. 661 x 483 mm.
Collection: Library, Royal Botanic Gardens, Kew.

During her journeys, Margaret Mee collected four of the five species of *Neoregalia* known from Amazonian Brazil, and is credited with first discovering three of them herself - N. *margaretae,* N. *leviana,* and N. *meeana.* Margaret's significant contribution to the knowledge of this genus helped establish her reputation as both a scientist and a botanical explorer. As *Neoregalia margaretae* has not yet been recollected, it is known only from Margaret's collections.

The plant in her painting was found in January of 1965 in a remote region of Amazonas – on the banks of the Rio Içana, a right bank tributary of the upper Rio Negro. The painting accurately depicts the splendor of N. *margaretae.* At its center are tiny blue and white flowers, set in a sunken cluster, surrounded by the brilliant, rose-colored inner leaves of the rosette, which retain their flush of color long after the flowers have died. The reservoir or tank formed by the leaves of the plant becomes filled with rain water, providing a home for a myriad of animal life, from tiny insects to small vertebrates such as frogs or lizards. Those that die serve as a source of nutrition for the plant as it absorbs the water and dissolved salts by means of its leaf scales.

Behind Salvador's cottage stood great trees on the fringe of virgin jungle...Maria informed me that no one would climb these trees, fearing the surucucu *(a venomous snake) so we moved away rapidly to a new hunting ground, and it was there that I saw a group of neoregalias in the fork of a tree. They were without flowers, and swarming with large, ferocious ants. Some months later, after my return to São Paulo, I noticed that the centre of this bromeliad was tinged with crimson. Slowly this area grew larger and more intense in colour. Then one day in the heart of this red rosette appeared a colony of small white flowers faintly tinged with pink, emerging from the water which always collects in the cup. During the months of heavy rainfall in Içana, the forests there will be studded with these magenta jewels.*

[M. Mee, **Flowers of the Brazilian Forest,** Plate 25]

Neoregelia leviana, 1968 (family Bromeliaceae)
Pencil and gouache on paper. 661 x 483 mm.
Collection: Library, Royal Botanic Gardens, Kew.

Neoregelia leviana is known scientifically only from Margaret Mee's collection of 1967 from the banks of the Rio Cauaburi, a left bank tributary of the Rio Negro. Her discovery of this species occurred during her attempted ascent of the famous Pico da Neblina mountain, which lies on the border with Venezuela. As long ago as the mid 1800's, the British explorer, Richard Spruce, had reported sighting a vast mountainous formation during his exploration of the upper Rio Negro. The first recorded ascent, eleven weeks of laborious trail cutting, did not occur until 1953 when it was led by Bassett Maguire, Curator of the New York Botanical Garden.

Intrigued by this mountainous region and assisted by a scientific grant from the National Geographic Society, Margaret Mee became, in 1967, the first woman to attempt a southern approach to this mountain. Torrential rains, however, obliterated the trail and the expedition had to be abandoned. An account of the journey with its botanical discoveries, including *Neoregalia leviana*, was presented in a special National Geographic Society Research Report.
(Inscribed on the lower right of the painting is the date 'Dec. 1964'. This conflicts with the dates of collection given here and in the original publication of the species.)

Small inlets and igapó broke the line of forest for almost a hundred miles...we...travelled upstream, the river narrowing as we passed with forest and igapó each side...I slept in my boat. Early in the morning...I found a bromeliad, Neoregelia leviana, a very beautiful specimen with fine plants forming a candelabra.

[M. Mee (edited T. Morrison),
**Margaret Mee: In Search of
Flowers of the Amazon Forests,**
Journey Four]

Neoregelia leviana, Margaret Mee field sketch

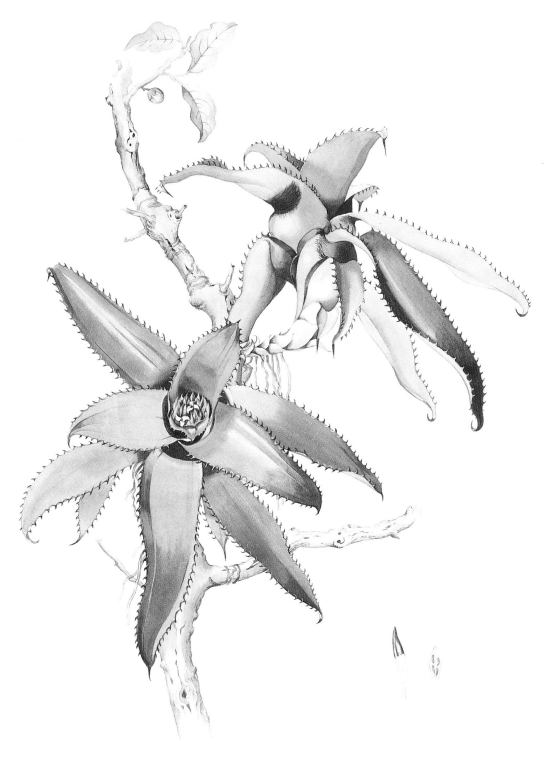

Margaret Mee

(Neoregelia tocantina)
Pico Amazonas, Rio
Uaupés Dec 1964
(Neoregelia eleutheropetala L.B. Smith 1967)

Neoreglia sp., 1965 (family Bromeliaceae)
Pencil and gouache on paper. 661 x 483 mm.
Collection: Library, Royal Botanic Gardens, Kew.

The genus *Neoregalia* was named in honor of the German botanist A.von Regel, superintendent of the Imperial Botanic Gardens, St. Petersburg, Russia. It has become a favorite indoor plant, particularly in Germany and Japan, as it is easy to maintain and produces dramatically colored foliage, often lasting months after the flowers have withered. In the wild, the plants grow epiphytically on lower branches of trees, seeking a shaded place with good air circulation.

This painting of a plant from the Rio Uaupés, Amazonas correctly depicts the tentacle-like nature of its pale-green, spiny leaves, delicately edged in rose, encompassing the more vibrantly red, inner leaves which border the inflorescence. Known from eastern Peru and Colombia, this genus is most abundant in eastern Brazil, particularly in the area known as the 'Mata Atlântica', the coastal forest region.

Neoregalia sp. (Neoregalia meeana), Margaret Mee field sketch

Aechmea sp.
Proc. Amazonas, Alto Rio
Negro, Brazil, Nov 1964

Neoregelia eleutheropetala, 1971 (family Bromeliaceae)
Pencil and gouache on paper. 661 x 483 mm.
Collection: Library, Royal Botanic Gardens, Kew.

Neoregalia eleutheropetala, first discovered in Peru in 1902, is the most widespread of the Amazonian neoregalias, distributed throughout the Amazonian regions of Colombia, Venezuela, Peru and Brazil. It can be found growing as an epiphyte or terrestrial in rainforests at altitudes ranging from 100 to 1650 meters.

The plant depicted in Margaret Mee's painting is from the Rio Urupadi, which flows across the border between the states of Pará and Amazonas. The compact rosette is formed by 30 or more, red and green banded leaves, creating the water tank or reservoir common amongst several genera of the *Bromeliaceae* family. Cupped in the center of its innermost leaves is the inflorescence, containing numerous tiny white flowers.

Today is the eighth day of the journey, and in view of the difficulties of landing to collect yesterday, I decided to try again today...Accompanied only by the faithful Bento, I found myself in a lovely backwater, a series of little bays surrounded by igapó, where the trees supported clusters of Schomburgkia orchids and various species of bromeliads. All my troubles vanished in the excitement of seeing the glowing scarlet leaves and olive green heart sparkling with pale violet florets, of Neoregelia eleutheropetala. Bento climbed into the tree cautiously, fearful of falling into the river, which here, he assured me, was a favourite haunt of the Sucuriju, the great Anaconda. When I returned to the friendly Mission in Maués, on my journey back to Manaus, I was invited to stay and to paint my plants in a disused schoolroom and was greeted by the sisters with apparent relief that I had survived the trip up the rivers.

[M. Mee, **Flowers of the Amazon,** Plate 6]

Neoregelia eleutheropetala, Margaret Mee field sketch

Billbergia decora, 1979 (family Bromeliaceae)
Pencil and gouache on paper. 661 x 483 mm.
Collection: Library, Royal Botanic Gardens, Kew.

Billbergia, a genus of approximately 60 species, is named after the Swedish botanist Gustav Johannes Billberg (1772-1844). These plants are tall and tubular and thus easily distinguishable from the characteristic rosette shape of the Aechmeas. Its five to eight leaves, fewer in number than most bromeliads, are usually mottled, banded, or variegated with contrasting color. Although its colorful, pendent inflorescence is short-lived, lasting only three to five days, it can bloom up to three times a year.

Billbergia decora was first collected in 1831 by the German botanist and explorer Eduard F. Poeppig. Its name is derived from the Latin *decoratus* (ornate), referring to the decorative nature of this plant so beautifully illustrated in Margaret Mee's painting. It grows as an epiphyte in the forests of Amazonian Peru, Bolivia, and Brazil. This species had not been recorded from the Rio Negro region until Margaret collected it in the Arquipelago das Anavilhanas, a network of river islands on the Rio Negro close to Manaus.

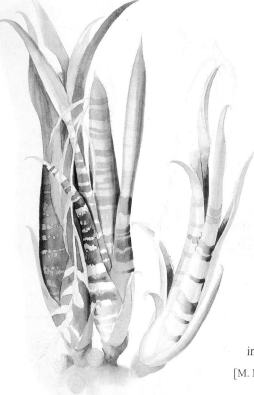

We are back on the Rio Negro, having just left the Paraná do Cantagalo. The forests look magnificent in the warm evening light...The river is glassy...We moored to a half submerged tree beside a steep bank on a wide stretch of the river...This morning the waters are still calm...I stopped next to collect more plants in the Arquipelago das Anavilhanas which from here lies beyond the mouth of Rio Jaú in the direction of Manaus, and which is to become a forest reserve. The sheltered waterways, fringed with magnificent trees, seem remotely distant from the Rio Negro where boats pass with irregular frequency. It was beside these tranquil waters that I found a Billbergia decora clinging to an aged tree covered with epiphytes. This lovely Billbergia consisted of a group of plants with three pendant spikes of flowers between whose curled green petals twisted the narrow pink bracts waving like silken ribbons in the faint breeze.

[M. Mee, **Flowers of the Amazon,** Plate 5]

Billbergia decora, Margaret Meed field sketch

Margaret Mee
Italy 1988

Billbergia decora Poepp & Endl
Orchid Cacti quadrangularis
Rio de Janeiro 1988

Selenicereus wittii, 1978 (family Cactaceae)
Pencil and gouache on paper. 730 x 507 mm.
Collection: Library, Royal Botanic Gardens, Kew.

The German botanist Karl Schumann (1891-1904), a 19th century leading expert on the
Cactaceae family, named this remarkable epiphytic cactus *Cereus wittii* in 1900, working from
specimens sent to him by a German collector, N.H.Witt, residing in Manaus at the time. In 1913,
the plant was placed in a genus by itself as *Strophocactus wittii,* the generic name from the word *strophe*
(twisting, curling) referring to the manner in which the flattened leaf-like stems wind themselves
around Amazonian trees. In 1986, taxonomists determined that this extraordinary night-
blooming cactus belonged in the *Selenicereus* genus, which includes the spectacular, night-flowering
cactus, *Selenicereus grandiflorus,* 'Queen of the Night'. The generic name is derived from the Greek
selene, meaning moon.

Margaret Mee collected this plant in the igapó (flooded forest) of the Arquipelago das
Anavilhanas, a reserve on the Rio Negro near Manaus. In this painting, Margaret's first of
the species, *Selenicereus wittii* is beautifully portrayed within its forest surroundings,
depicting its developing fruit and curious spine-edged, flattened stems, suffused
with crimson.

Morning dawned bright and clear after a heavy fall of rain in the night, so we took the
canoe and Pedro and I paddled to a marvellous lake, one of many, in the Archipelago of
Anavilhanas. There, epiphytes grew in profusion on the giant trees...Many years ago
I had collected a thorny, red-leafed cactus from the igapó... Years later I had
found this same species again on the Rio Daraá, a tributary of the Alto Rio
Negro, and had discovered the name to be Strophocactus wittii.
Scientists working in Manaus had told me that this plant had been found
recently in the area of Anavilhanas, and as we penetrated deeper into
the igapó, I caught sight of the brilliant scarlet leaves, high on a
tree trunk...This strange cactus has its roots on the under side of
the leaf where they grow from the veins; thus it clings close to the
bark of the tree and appears almost like a design in low relief.
Partially immersed in the black waters for about six months of the
year, it emerges when the water level falls, and eventually remains
high above the waterline, when it flowers and fruits.

[M. Mee, **Flowers of the Amazon,** Plate 24]

Selenicereus wittii, Margaret Mee field sketch

Margaret Mee (signature)

Selenicereus wittii, 1981 (family Cactaceae)
Pencil and gouache on paper. 730 x 507 mm.
Collection: Library, Royal Botanic Gardens, Kew.

Margaret Mee's series of paintings of *Selenicereus wittii* is the only known study of this plant in the wild. Several paintings of the related species, *Selenicereus grandiflorus*, all drawn from cultivated plants, have become quite famous. As early as 1752, the celebrated flower painter, Georg Dionysius Ehret, beautifully portrayed this cactus, entitling it, 'Queen of the Night'. A painting by the renowned Belgian artist, Pierre-Joseph Redoute dating from the time of Marie Antoinette, also depicted this night-flowering cactus. However, this *Selenicereus* species is probably best known from the painting entitled 'The Night Blowing Cereus', included in Robert Thornton's magnificent folio, *The Temple of Flora*, published in parts, from 1797 to 1807.

Selenicereus wittii occurs in the Brazilian Amazonian region, where it thrives in the igapó, permanently flooded swamp forest. Margaret had initially noted this rare cactus during her early explorations in 1964, and again on three other occasions, but always without flowers. This painting portrays plants which had flowered the previous night. As a result, the flowers are already withering.

After excursions to different parts of the archipelago, I began to consider that we must continue to search the igapó as the sparse botanical information suggested this was the place to find the strophocactus I sought...Sue, who had been paddling the canoe in the nearby igarapé, came back greatly excited at having found leaves of this very plant...Not only did I see a long strand of scarlet leaves growing flat against the tree trunk, but two large flower buds were just within Sue's reach! The stalks of the flowers were very long, about twelve inches, and the sepals reddish green; the petals were white, not red as I had been led to believe...Every day after this discovery we visited the igarapé, watching the flowers and waiting for them to open...The next morning... we paddled slowly and found the plant was unchanged except for the remaining bud. The flower was half open with its delicate petals carefully entwined... The flower had opened and closed overnight... one brief night of glorious show. Flowering was over, and all I could do was to think of searching again in another year.

[M. Mee (edited T. Morrison), **Margaret Mee: In Search of Flowers of the Amazon Forests,** Journey Fifteen]

Selenicereus wittii, Margaret Mee field sketch

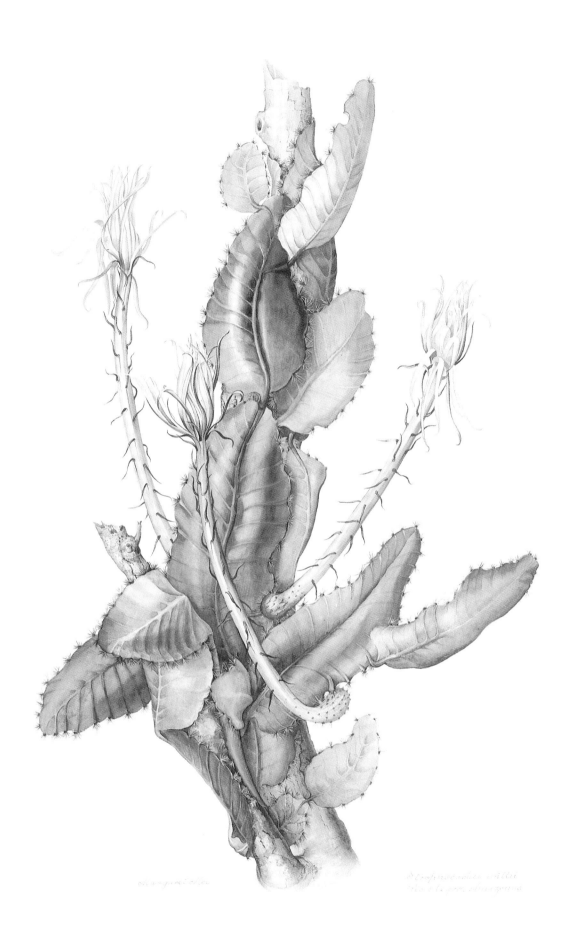

Selenicereus wittii, 1988 (family Cactaceae)
Pencil and gouache on paper. 730 x 507 mm.
Collection: Mr. Greville Mee

After first seeing this fascinating, night-flowering cactus in 1964, Margaret began a search that eventually grew to span twenty-four years - to find and paint the 'Moonflower' in full bloom. Finally, in May of 1988, the month of her 79th birthday and barely six months before her untimely death, Margaret had the thrill, during an all-night vigil, of witnessing the beauty of the delicate, fragrant flower in full bloom, and of sketching it by torchlight from the deck of a riverboat in the *igapó* of the forest reserve, Arquipelago das Anavilhanas, Rio Negro.

Each flower of *Selenicereus wittii* is in the form of a very long tube that flares out at the end, creating a large, white ephemeral blossom that opens at night, lasting only till the dawn of the next morning. As with several other species of the genus, the tubular shape of the flower and its night-blooming habit has led experts to believe that this epiphytic cactus is pollinated by long-tongued hawkmoths.

We had been waiting almost two hours and the buds had not changed...As I stood there with the dim outline of the forest all around I was spellbound. Then the first petal began to move and then another as the flower burst into life. It was opening so quickly. A chair was passed to the roof, and Sally found the rest of my sketching materials whilst Sue stood beside me with a small portable battery light...The flower was nearly open but the strong photographic lights seemed to slow down the opening, so I begged that the light be dimmed, and we continued with only a faint illumination and the light of the full moon rising over the darkened rim of forest. In the early stages an extraordinary sweet perfume wafted from the flower, and we were all transfixed by the beauty of the delicate and unexpectedly large bloom...Our vigil was long and I conclude that our intrusion had deterred the pollinator, upsetting the delicate balance between the plant and the animal which has taken tens of millions of years to evolve...With the dawn the flower closed and we watched fascinated and humbled by the experience.

[M. Mee, (edited T. Morrison) **Margaret Mee: In Search of Flowers of the Amazon Forests,** Journey Fifteen]

Margaret Mee
June 1988

Rudolfiella aurantiaca, 1971 (family Orchidaceae)
Pencil and gouache on paper. 661 x 483 mm.
Collection: Library, Royal Botanic Gardens, Kew.

In 1836, the celebrated British botanist John Lindley described *Rudolfiella aurantiaca* from a plant collected in Guyana, which flowered in the collection of the Duke of Devonshire at Chiswick, London. The Duke, a man of tremendous wealth, was well known at the time for his conservatory in Chatsworth, Derbyshire, home to one of the largest orchid collections of that time.

This painting depicts the plant as Margaret Mee observed it, perched on a Jará palm in the igapó (flooded) forests of the Rio Negro, a common habitat for this epiphytic orchid. Bearing up to twenty, golden yellow, red-spotted flowers, the inflorescence of this striking plant may reach 30 cm. long. It is widely distributed in the Amazonian area of Brazil, Peru, Colombia, Venezuela and the Guianas.

We...were moving rapidly up the dark waters of the Rio Negro, which were lapping lazily against the white sands of the caatinga forests fringed with Jará palms...Orchids grow in profusion on the stems of the Jará palm, weaving their roots into the fibrous bark. It was on such a palm that I found Rudolfiella aurantiaca, full of flowers and buds. The perfumed yellow flowers are spotted with chestnut brown and the slightly hexagonal bulbs are pin spotted with the same colour. I made some drawings and colour notes, seated in the boat, fearing that the delicate flowers would not weather the return journey...Since that day I have found this orchid on other tributaries of the Rio Negro, Rio Cuiuni, Rio Jaú, and black water rivers where the Jará palms abound. But now, with the destruction of the forests and igapó it is becoming scarce and one has to travel far afield to find it.

[M. Mee, **Flowers of the Amazon,** Plate 19]

Oncidium lanceanum, 1975 (family Orchidaceae)
Pencil and gouache on paper. 661 x 483 mm.
Collection: Library, Royal Botanic Gardens, Kew.

As a member of the so-called 'Mule-ear' orchids, this plant is distinctive for its erect, leathery leaves, finely mottled with red to chocolate-brown coloring. The genus *Oncidium* is extensive, containing over 400 species of epiphytes and has remained one of the most widely cultivated and popular genera throughout the years. John Lindley described this species in 1836, dedicating it to John H. Lance, who introduced it into cultivation from Surinam.

Collected along the banks of the upper Rio Negro, this plant bears twenty or more long-lasting, intensely fragrant flowers, whose scent is reminiscent of cloves. These striking flowers, with a diameter of about four cm. vary in color from yellow to yellow-green and can be found in Venezuela, Trinidad, the Guianas, and Amazonas state in Brazil.

It was in the Boca do Rio Cuiuni de Cima that I found the most interesting plants of my journey on that river...On the day before returning, I found the plants of an Oncidium which looked like Oncidium lanceanum in the great macucuzinho tree, but without flowers. There was a splendid Billbergia too, out of which jumped a very large frog, and later in the day two red scorpions emerged from the same plant...Then in the igapó we passed under the discarded skin of a large snake, hanging from the trees like a gossamer liana.

[M. Mee, **Flowers of the Amazon,** Plate 18]

Oncidium sp., 1985 (family Orchidaceae)
Pencil and gouache on paper. 661 x 483 mm.
Collection: Library, Royal Botanic Gardens, Kew.

The name *Oncidium* is derived from the Greek word *onkos* (swelling or mass), undoubtedly referring to the characteristic warty callus on the lip of many of the species. It was described in Stockholm by the Swedish botanist Olaf Swartz in 1800. Swartz authored several seminal works on orchid morphology in the late 1700's, having been educated at Uppsala as a student of Linnaeus's son.

Margaret Mee's painting of this delicate orchid is based on a plant from Amazonas state. The species remains undescribed by taxonomists.

Catasetum saccatum, 1977 (family Orchidaceae)
Pencil and gouache on paper. 661 x 483 mm.
Collection: Library, Royal Botanic Gardens, Kew.

The genus *Catasetum* confused taxonomists for many years mainly because of the dimorphic flowers of many of its species. Plants that produced female flowers and a number of others that produced hermaphrodite flowers (both male and female organs in the same flower) were placed in different genera from those that produced only male flowers. After much study, Charles Darwin, in the *Journal of the Linnaean Society* (1862), concluded that they all belonged to the same genus and in certain instances to the same species.

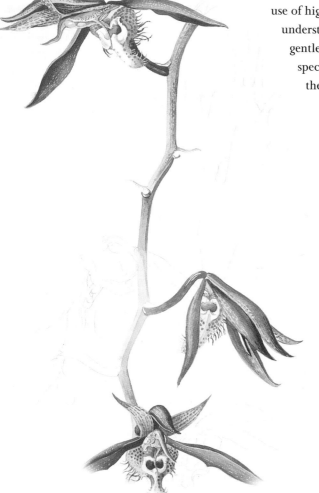

Note the yellow-green female flowers and the more numerous maroon to brown male ones. With her skillful use of highlights and shadows, Margaret allows one to understand the thick texture of the flowers and the gentle curves of the leaves. This highly variable species is distributed throughout Peru, Brazil, and the Guianas.

A large room was assigned to me constructed like the rest of the maloca [large Indian house], of slender posts and palm leaves…The light was very dim, but I managed to paint the plants which I had collected in the nearby igapó, most spectacular of which was Catasetum saccatum. The masculine flowers of this strangely beautiful plant are completely different from the female flowers, imitating dark bats with outspread wings. The long pendent stem supported more than fifteen blooms. The modest female flowers resemble the green hoods of elfins, growing on an erect stem. Both forms grow on the same plant and even from the same pseudo-bulb. Until Charles Darwin pronounced them to be the same species, they were considered to be different plants.

[M. Mee, **Flowers of the Amazon,** Plate 16]

Catasetum saccatum, Margaret Mee field sketch

Margaret Mee   Catasetum saccatum Lindl.   Amazonas
1977

Catasetum barbatum, 1975 (family Orchidaceae)
Pencil and gouache on paper. 661 x 483 mm.
Collection: Library, Royal Botanic Gardens, Kew.

A hairy lip characterizes this epiphytic orchid; hence its Latin name meaning *'bearded Catasetum'*. A widely distributed species, it flourishes from the northeast of Brazil to Bolivia, through the Guyanas, Venezuela, Colombia and Peru. It was discovered in Guyana by John Henchman, who collected for the nursery of Messrs. Low & Co. of Clapton, London.

In the 1836 issue of the *Botanical Register*, John Lindley initially described the male flowers of this species as *Myanthus barbatu*, but upon the realization that this species produces both male and female flowers, he transferred it to the *Catasetum* genus in 1844.

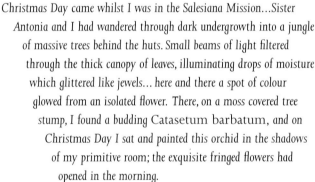

Christmas Day came whilst I was in the Salesiana Mission...Sister Antonia and I had wandered through dark undergrowth into a jungle of massive trees behind the huts. Small beams of light filtered through the thick canopy of leaves, illuminating drops of moisture which glittered like jewels... here and there a spot of colour glowed from an isolated flower. There, on a moss covered tree stump, I found a budding Catasetum barbatum, and on Christmas Day I sat and painted this orchid in the shadows of my primitive room; the exquisite fringed flowers had opened in the morning.

[M. Mee, **Flowers of the Brazilian Forests,** Plate 15]

Catasetum barbatum, Margaret Mee field sketch

Catasetum barbatum
Lindl.
Amazonas, Rio Cuini

Catasetum appendiculatum, 1985 (family Orchidaceae)
Pencil and gouache on paper. 661 x 483 mm.
Collection: Library, Royal Botanic Gardens, Kew.

This rare Brazilian orchid belongs in the *Catasetum cristatum* complex, being characterized by the lip, which is ciliate or covered with fleshy hairs. It is easily distinguished from the better known C. *cristatum* and C. *barbatum* as its flowers are rose red, rather than the green of the former. The species was first described by Rudolf Schlechter in 1925.

Margaret is exquisitely precise in her treatment of the flowers. In addition, she has most successfully depicted the weight of the pendulous inflorescence upon the fragile stem.

...the journey to Içana was made by launch...I was given the Santa Casa as living quarters. The Indians preferred to sleep together, even though the room was somewhat over-crowded. But the room that I had was sad, and rather dark...the little Catasetum, which was already in bud when I found it at one of the brief stops on our river journey, in the dark forest behind an Indian hut, burst into fringy flowers. (Catasetum appendiculatum)

[Excerpt from Margaret Mee's Journals]

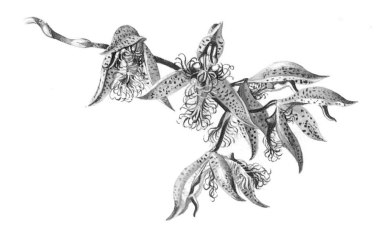

Catasetum appendiculatum, Margaret Mee field sketch

Catasetum appendiculatum
Rio Negro, Amazonas

Margaret Mee
May 1965

Catasetum macrocarpum, August 1981 (family Orchidaceae)
Pencil and gouache on paper. 661 x 483 mm.
Collection: Library, Royal Botanic Gardens, Kew.

Possibly the most common species of *Catasetum* in cultivation, *Catasetum macrocarpum* is distributed throughout Columbia, Venezuela, the Guianas and Brazil. This specimen produced exclusively male flowers of dark green to yellowish-green, spotted with maroon, with the interior surface of the helmet-shaped lip being particularly eye-catching in its coloration.

A strong wind is driving against us as we dip and toss across the vast lakes... Just at the peak of the storm, I caught sight of a magnificent Catasetum in flower high on the trunk of a large tree. Before it lay a great barrier of floating grass...So Manoel, who was familiar with these grass 'islands', took the canoe and, with the paddle, fought his way through until he reached the tree. He was just able to reach the orchid, detaching it with the blade. It is a beautiful Catasetum macrocarpum. An absolutely gorgeous plant, and I must paint it soon...

[M. Mee (edited T. Morrison), **Margaret Mee: In Search of Flowers of the Amazon Forests,** Journey Nine]

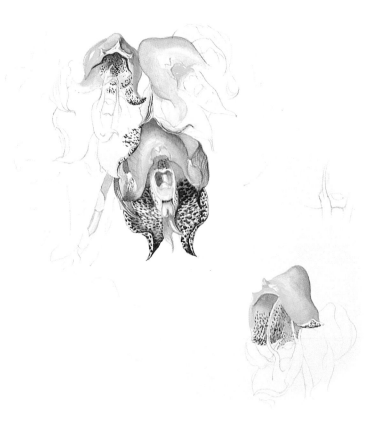

Catasetum macrocarpum, Margaret Mee field sketch

Margaret Mee

Catasetum macrocarpum, July 1981 (family Orchidaceae)
Pencil and gouache on paper. 661 x 483 mm.
Collection: Library, Royal Botanic Gardens, Kew.

The genus *Catasetum*, first described by Carl Kunth in 1820, contains over 60 known species distributed in Central and South America and the West Indies. Its name is derived from the Greek *kata* (down) and the Latin *seta* (bristle), referring to the two antenna-like projections on the column of the male flower. These antennae are sensitive to touch, releasing the pollinia (pollen masses) explosively onto the back of specific bee pollinators. Through a complex process, often involving mimicry, pollination occurs when the insect visits another flower and the pollinia is deposited on its stigmatic surface.

This plant, also a *Catasetum macrocarpum* as in the previous painting, depicts the more fleshy, greenish-yellow female flowers. Margaret has been particularly successful in capturing the high gloss characteristic of the lip of the female flower.

Catasetum macrocarpum, Margaret Mee field sketch

Margaret Mee

Catasetum galeritum, 1981 (family Orchidaceae)
Pencil and gouache on paper. 661 x 483 mm.
Collection: Library, Royal Botanic Gardens, Kew

This species was first described in 1886 by the eminent orchidologist H.G. Reichenbach, from whom is quoted, "I have at hand an inflorescence of seven flowers, which are nearly half as large again as *Catasetum atratum* ... the flowers are conspicuous in their bright color and look rather pretty for those of *Catasetum*".

This species was first illustrated in *Lindenia* in 1886 from a plant introduced by *Continentale d'Horticulture*, probably originating from Brazil. It is a rare species about which very little has been recorded.

We moored beside the trunk of a fallen tree on which grew orchids, including a Catasetum, the first I had seen in this area. I climbed into the canoe and edged my way under the arch formed by the toppled trunks. Standing up in the dugout - a rather precarious balancing act at the best of times - I tried to detach the plant with my bush knife. The movement disturbed a small wasp's nest nearby and without warning the creatures attacked. I felt a sharp pain in the neck, and then another on my bare wrist. Stunned I fell into the canoe moaning 'Caba!' The stings were agonizing and from then on I understood why the caboclos are so terrified of cabas. But not so Joao and José, for when my pain had subsided slightly and I was prepared to try again to get the Catasetum, they intervened. Despite my protestations and even though they got close to the angry wasps, they very carefully and cautiously detached the orchid without getting one sting.
[M. Mee, (edited T. Morrison), **Margaret Mee: In Search of Flowers of the Amazon Forests,** Journey Eleven]

Catasetum fimbriatum, 1982 (family Orchidaceae)
Pencil and gouache on paper. 661 x 483 mm.
Collection: Library, Royal Botanic Gardens, Kew.

Discovered in the Brazilian State of São Paulo, near Villa Franca, *Catasetum fimbriatum* was first introduced into cultivation by J. de Jonghe in 1847. Based on the identification of the male flowers, the orchidologist C. Morren first described the plant as *Myanthus fimbriatus* in 1848, but it was subsequently transferred to the genus *Catasetum* in 1850 by John Lindley in Paxton's *Flower Garden*.

This epiphytic plant is distributed throughout Venezuela, Paraguay, Argentina, Bolivia, and Brazil, where it flowers with an arching spike up to 45 cm. long, supporting seven to fifteen variable blooms. The plant in this painting, collected from the upper Rio Juruena in Mato Grosso, depicts the dull, yellow-green female flowers, rather outshone by the more handsome male flowers that are pale green and streaked with red-purple markings, with deeply fringed lips.

...I went collecting by canoe with Raimundo. It was gloriously peaceful paddling along the river to a rocky little island where I found some remarkable catasetums, or orchids, with huge seed pods. Beside them some wasps had made tiny nests of a substance like paper mache, each a beautiful little pot with a lid which opened neatly.
[M. Mee, (edited T. Morrison) **Margaret Mee: In Search of Flowers of the Amazon Forests,** Journey Two]

Catasetum punctatum, 1974 (family Orchidaceae)
Pencil and gouache on paper. 661 x 483 mm.
Collection: Library, Royal Botanic Gardens, Kew.

Catasetum punctatum, a rare epiphytic orchid, was introduced into cultivation by Messrs. Linden's *L'Horticulture Internationale* and flowered for the first time in the company's greenhouses in Brussels. Jean Linden (1817-98) had spent ten years as a collector of rare orchids and other plants for both the Belgian government and private individuals before establishing his own nursery in Ghent with his son Lucien in the mid-1800's. After moving to Brussels, this firm became one of the most successful in Europe, and Linden went on to support exploration of South America by financing a number of profitable expeditions in search of new and rare orchids.

This striking species was first illustrated in *Lindenia* in 1895. Its flowers, prominently carried on an arched inflorescence, are relatively large with a diameter up to six cm., and are reported to be highly fragrant. Margaret's painting is of a plant collected along the Rio Mamori, near Manaus, Amazonas.

Leaving the silent forest behind, we ran into rough waters on the open river, which made further collecting impossible. So we sought shelter in the narrow Furo do Cucu which led to the igapó of Tucumanduba. There the surface of the water was like a mirror, and reality and reflections were almost indistinguishable one from the other. Orchids and bromeliads grew there in profusion, and amongst them I was fortunate enough to find Catasetum punctatum. The large flower never opens fully; it has a projecting labellum, pale silver-green petals on the outer side, and a deep purple interior. The inflorescence of seven flowers hung semi-pendent from the robust pseudo-bulb, being secured to a rotting branch by a massive tangle of roots. I was able to paint these flowers before the light faded, after which we supped on piranhas...

[M. Mee, **Flowers of the Amazon,**, Plate 15]

Catasetum punctatum, Margaret Mee field sketch

Epidendrum punctatum Rolfe
Amazonas, Rio Mamoré

Margaret Mee
July, 1974

Margaret Mee

Catasetum sp., 1972 (family Orchidaceae)
Pencil and gouache on paper. 661 x 483 mm.
Collection: Library, Royal Botanic Gardens, Kew.

Note the weathered branch on which this unnamed *Catasetum* orchid from the Rio Negro is perched. Margaret was clearly fascinated by the curious shapes and textures of the trees and branches in the *igapó* (flooded forest), home to many of the epiphytic plants that she collected and portrayed in her paintings. A number of her exquisite field sketches are detailed pencil studies of these weather-sculpted structures. Margaret Mee's drawings are now considered as impressive a part of her artistic legacy as her finished paintings.

It was about nine o'clock in the morning...time enough to collect in the igapó before the heat became too intense. So, after slinging my hammock, and stacking up my baggage in the little room where I was to spend the night...I went paddling up the river in a small canoe...Of course, climbing a tree directly from a canoe is a problem, and a danger to the passengers, as branches fall in around the boat. Sometimes snakes and lizards fall in too. A beautiful little lizard fell into our canoe when one of the boys climbed up a tree to get a Catasetum that I had spotted.

[Excerpt from Margaret Mee's Journals]

Catasetum sp.
Natural hybrid ?
Amazonas, Rio Negro 1842 ?

Margaret Mee

Margaret Mee

Catasetum discolor, 1981 (family Orchidaceae)
Pencil and gouache on paper. 661 x 483 mm.
Collection: Library, Royal Botanic Gardens, Kew.

This beautiful species of the *Catasetum* family, described by the orchidologist John Lindley in the *Botanical Register* in 1854, is a medium-sized plant that can be either terrestrial or epiphytic in its habit of growth. It has strap-shaped leaves and produces up to twenty-five flowers on a gently arched inflorescence. The flowers of both sexes appear to be quite similar. However, the male flowers are known to be smaller than the female in this species.

Distributed throughout Colombia, the Guianas, Venezuela, Peru and Brazil, *Catasetum discolor* flowers from February to July. The flowers are commonly yellowish-green, often tinged with lilac, but occur in a range of color forms, with each variety having its own names, e.g., *C. discolor* var. *roseo-album*. Margaret collected this plant from the Rio Maraú, near Maués, Amazonas.

After Sao Felipe, a simple village of a few thatched huts, we chugged onwards through the most lush and tropical region I had ever seen. Jungle seemed to merge into river, for tree trunk, lianas, roots and foliage were inseparable from their reflections; it was a picture of luxuriant vegetation, where the igarapés were transformed into dark, mysterious tunnels through the forest... I hung my hammock in the airless boat above piles of cargo, for there was little free space. Above me, in my straw hat, a little Catasetum which I had found on the way was bursting into flower.

[M. Mee, (edited T. Morrison)
**Margaret Mee: In Search of Flowers
of the Amazon Forests,** Journey Three]

Catasetum discolor, Margaret Mee field sketch

Ionopsis utricularioides, 1984 (family Orchidaceae)
Pencil and gouache on paper. 661 x 483 mm.
Collection: Library, Royal Botanic Gardens, Kew.

Related to *Oncidium*, this elegant species has been known to botanists since the eighteenth century, when it was first described in 1788 as *Epidendrum utricularioides*. Some thirty years later, in 1821, the British botanist John Lindley transferred it to the genus *Ionopsis*, whose name was derived from the two Greek words, *ion* (violet) and *opsis* (appearance), referring to the similarity of its delicate flowers to violets. Although there are approximately ten species in this genus, *Ionopsis utricularioides* is the only one that is widely recognized.

Though it is widespread throughout tropical and subtropical America, even reaching as far as Florida, *Ionopsis utricularioides* is not known from western Amazonia. Usually epiphytic, these plants can commonly be found growing in maté and guava trees up to 800 meters elevation. It produces flower spikes typically about 40 cm. long, carrying flowers that are variable in color from white to lilac to rose-red, with a striking magenta blotch on the lip. Margaret collected this plant on the beautiful Cuminá-mirum river in the state of Pará.

Plant hunting along the river banks is well nigh impossible in a big and clumsy boat, and to enter the igapó in Santana was out of the question. I was even more upset by the lack of a canoe, as we passed fascinating plants without a hope of getting near enough to identify them...A cabocla who came from the hut with a little boy, paddling her canoe, spoke to me in a friendly way and arranged to take me into the nearest igapó... We paddled among trees and bushes recently devastated by fire, though their wounds had begun to heal, and I found plants which had escaped the conflagration. There were orchids in plenty, the prize of them being Ionopsis utricularioides, with a mass of fragile violet flowers.

[M. Mee, (edited T. Morrison) **Margaret Mee: In Search of Flowers of the Amazon Forests,** Journey Thirteen]

Ionopsis utricularioides, Margaret Mee field sketch

Ionopsis utricularioides Lindl.
Ris brunosa—Mirim, Pará

Margaret Mee
August 1964

Sobralia margaritae 1977 (family Orchidaceae)
Pencil and gouache on paper. 661 x 483 mm.
Collection: Library, Royal Botanic Gardens, Kew.

Attractive foliage, distinctive flowers, and reedlike stems, up to 180 cm tall in some species, are all characteristic of the genus *Sobralia*. It was first described by H. Ruiz and J. Pavon in 1794 in honor of their friend Francisco Sobral, a Spanish physician and botanist during the latter years of the eighteenth century. Restricted to the tropics of Mexico and Central and South America, this genus includes approximately 35 species.

First discovered by Margaret Mee, who saw it growing on tall trees in the igapó (flooded forest) of the Rio Urupadi in Amazonas, *Sobralia margaritae* was named in her honour by her friend Guido F.J. Pabst, Brazil's premier orchid specialist. This fine epiphyte combines shiny, heavily veined leaves with large, finely-textured flowers, strongly resembling the showy flowers of the *Cattleya* genus in form. Although the flowers of *Sobralia margaritae* are short-lived, with some lasting only a day, the plant does continues to flower over a period of time.

During the month of May the waters of Rio Maués are high, and that year had risen higher than usual which made navigation difficult as the land was flooded for miles around; consequently we were trapped many times in pathless forests from which we escaped only through Severino's care and experience. Eventually he found his way into a tributary of the river, Rio Amena, and thence into a lovely igarapé where low palms growing in the water covered it with a blue haze and from their midst rose trees like columns in a Gothic cathedral. I scanned these trees for epiphytes, and on one of the tallest saw, with excitement, a huge wreath of orchids encircling the trunk. It was a Sobralia, without a doubt, and a giant of that genus...They were without flowers, but later it flowered and was found to be a new species and was named Sobralia margaritae.

[M. Mee, **Flowers of the Amazon,** Plate 17]

Sobralia margaritae, Margaret Mee field sketch

Zygosepalum labiosum, 1976 (family Orchidaceae)
Pencil and gouache on paper. 661 x 483 mm.
Collection: Library, Royal Botanic Gardens, Kew.

Zygosepalum, a small genus of possibly five species of orchids, was described in 1863 by H. G. Reichenbach (1823-1889), a German botanist and successor to John Lindley as the leading orchid taxonomist of the day. The generic name was derived from the Greek words *zygon* (yoke) and *sepalum* (sepal), probably referring to the fused sepals that are characteristic of the plants in this genus.

Growing epiphytically at elevations from 100 to 500 meters, *Zygosepalum labiosum* is frequently found in lowland forests. Its fragrant, long-lasting flowers, up to five cm. wide, are large in relation to the rest of the plant and handsome, with their white coloration and peachy-brown highlights. The painting clearly depicts the swollen stems, or pseudobulbs, remarkable adaptations that allow the plant to withstand the daily period of relative drought caused in the forest canopy by the sun.

The boat chugged heavily across Lago Jacupá...Sometimes we used the canoe to visit isolated places on the small streams and I was disturbed to find that people and houses were spread everywhere through the forest, much of it cleared...I was thankful when we returned to the canoe. We rejoined the river by tracing devious channels, and in one shady copse, massed on the mossy trees, gleamed the delicate white flowers of a rare orchid, Zygosepalum labiosum, *of which I eagerly collected a plant or two. Still gliding silently we passed unnoticed by a handsome iguana fully three feet long, green, black and grey, gracefully draped over the thick foliage in the canopy of a tree.*

[M. Mee,(edited T. Morrison)
Margaret Mee: In Search of Flowers of the Amazon Forests, Journey Thirteen]

Zygosepalum labiosum, Margaret Mee field sketch

Zygopetalum rostratum
L. C. Rich. spray
Para

Margaret Mee

Gongora maculata, 1959 (family Orchidaceae)
Pencil and gouache on paper. 661 x 483 mm.
Collection: Library, Royal Botanic Gardens, Kew.

Gongora is a small genus with upwards of a dozen species, with flowers of extremely variable coloration. Not widely hybridized, they are often grown for their unique flowers that are both attractive and lightly fragrant. The plants grow epiphytically, inhabiting ant nests in wet forest, with all species being pollinated very specifically by male euglossine bees. It is widely distributed from Mexico to Peru and Brazil, with this plant collected along the Rio Gurupi on Margaret's first journey to Amazonia.

Gongora maculata, also known as *Gongora quinquenervis,* was first described in 1798, with the genus named in honor of Don Antonio Cabballero y Gongora, viceroy of New Granada (Colombia and Ecuador) during the eighteenth century. The delicate balance of this plant and its placement on the page clearly illustrate Margaret's remarkable sense of design. The succulent pseudobulbs and crisp dark leaves, while seeming to float near the top of the page as if caught on a tree limb, securely anchor the pendulous inflorescence: grace and gravity at work in perfect unison.

Pingafogo was wonderful for collecting and I had already found the brilliant red spikes of the rare Heliconia glauca of the banana family, the white bells of the lily-like Eucharis amazonica, and the silvery leaves of a climber, Philodendron melinonii. My greatest find was the beautiful orchid, Gongora maculata, with a perfume like a hundred lilies.

[M. Mee (edited T. Morrison), **Margaret Mee: In Search of Flowers of the Amazon Forests,** Journey One]

Cochleanthes amazonica, 1978 (family Orchidaceae)
Pencil and gouache on paper. 661 x 483 mm.
Collection: Library, Royal Botanic Gardens, Kew.

The genus *Cochleanthes* was first described by Constantine S. Rafinesque in 1838 , who derived its name from the Greek words *cochlos* (shell) and *anthos* (flower), in reference to the shell-like appearance of its flowers. The approximately fifteen species that comprise this genus grow as epiphytes in cloud forests at elevations from 500 to 1,500 meters, and flower in succession throughout the greater part of the year.

The species *Cochleanthes amazonica* produces the largest flowers in the genus, reaching up to seven cm. in diameter. Its distinctive, single-flowered inflorescences, white with blue vein-lines on the lip, are often hidden among the leaves as the plants tend to form large clumps. A little-known species, its distribution seems quite restricted, with records from the Rio Marãnón in Peru and western Amazonas in Brazil. No specimens exist at Kew.

Margaret Mee
September 1748

Cochleanthes amazonica
(Rchb. f. & Warsc.)

Margaret Mee

Encyclia randii, 1983 (family Orchidaceae)
Pencil and gouache on paper. 750 x 507mm.
Collection: Library, Royal Botanic Gardens, Kew.

The distinguished explorer and botanist Joseph Dalton Hooker, who later became Director of the Royal Botanic Gardens, Kew, established the genus *Encyclia* in the *Botanical Magazine* in 1828. He derived its name from the Greek *enkyklein* (to encircle), referring to the way in which the lip encloses the column. It is a genus of more than 240 species of mostly epiphytic plants, usually found in seasonally dry forest from sea level up to 1,000 meters elevation and distributed throughout tropical America.

Encyclia randii, a Brazilian species, was discovered in the last century by Edward Rand on the Rio Solimões and subsequently named by the celebrated Brazilian botanist, João Barbosa Rodrigues. Its distribution extends from western Amazonas to the eastern state of Pernambuco.

Margaret Mee
1965

Encyclia randii (Barb. Rodr.)
Amazonas   Porto d Brade

Cattleya violacea, 1981 (family Orchidaceae)
Pencil and gouache on paper. 661 x 483 mm.
Collection: Library, Royal Botanic Gardens, Kew.

The genus *Cattleya*, containing approximately sixty species of beautiful tropical American orchids, is one of the most widely grown genera in the orchid family. The plants were first introduced into England in 1818, arriving in a crate from Brazil with the leaves of *Cattleya* orchids serving as a protective outer wrapping for lichens and mosses. It was William Cattley, the notable British horticulturist, who recognized the plants as unusual, nurturing them until they flowered in 1824. The distinguished botanist John Lindley later established it as a new genus and dedicated it to Cattley.

Cattleya violacea was first discovered on the Rio Orinoco in Venezuela by Alexander von Humboldt and his companion Aimé Bonpland during their celebrated journey to the Americas between 1799 and 1804. The striking, rose-purple flowers of this orchid are delightfully fragrant and long-lasting. This painting is a fine example of Margaret Mee's ability to combine botanical accuracy with her remarkable flair for composition. The *Cattleya*, shown in its natural habitat of igapó forest, is accompanied by the aquatic aroid, *Urospatha sagittifolia*, the epiphytic *Clusia* in the foreground, and down below, the new inflorescences of *Heliconia* plants.

Further afield we encountered an igapó of a very different character; gaunt, dried out trees, some of considerable height, reared amongst a tangle of vegetation. They were laden with epiphytes, but some of the trees were so rotten that it was impossible to climb them. In spite of this I brought out a fine collection of plants, including catasetums, brassavolas and a marvellous Cattleya *orchid -* Cattleya violacea, *with fine blooms.*

[M. Mee, (edited T. Morrison) **Margaret Mee: In Search of Flowers of the Amazon Forests,** Journey Six]

Cattleya violacea, Margaret Mee field sketch

Margaret Mee
1981

Cattleya violacea
Rio Curni, Amazonas

Mormodes buccinator, 1975 (family Orchidaceae)
Pencil and gouache on paper. 661 x 483 mm.
Collection: Library, Royal Botanic Gardens, Kew.

The unique twists of the column and lip of the genus *Mormodes* amazed the eminent taxonomist John Lindley in 1836, prompting him to coin its generic name from the Greek word *mormo* (phantom, frightful object). Distributed from Mexico to Bolivia and Brazil, these epiphytic orchids, also known as *Mormodes amazonica*, often occur on dead limbs of trees in moist or wet forests, at elevations from sea level to 800 meters. Like their relatives the *Catasetums Mormodes* flowers may be unisexual and the shape of their flowers may be extremely variable within a single species.

Eventually we landed on a wonderful white beach...
We filled the canoe with plants and moved slowly and
silently through the beautiful igapó, where the sweet
scented Curupitá flowers attracted hosts of glittering
hummingbirds, and we had to take shelter to steer clear
of the tiny nests suspended from the slenderest stems
hanging over the water. An old tree stump served as a
nest for one speckled egg guarded jealously by a chestnut
coloured Tree Creeper. It was an enchanted paradise; long
may it so remain. Then Mormodes amazonica came
to view, growing in the company of Catasetum
gnomus.

[M. Mee, **Flowers of the Amazon,** Plate 21]

Mormodes buccinator, Margaret Mee field sketch

Mormodes buccinator, 1975 (family Orchidaceae)
Pencil and gouache on paper. 661 x 483 mm.
Collection: Library, Royal Botanic Gardens, Kew.

Mormodes buccinator was first described by the distinguished British orchidologist, John Lindley in 1840 and is distributed from Mexico to Equador, Venezuela and Brazil, where it is restricted to the state of Amazonas. It can often be found growing on dead trees up to 1,500 meters above sea level. Flowering from winter to spring, it produces an erect to arching spike 15-40 cm. long on which numerous fleshy flowers are borne. They appear in a variety of colors, from white - like the plant pictured here - to greenish-yellow, yellow, pale pink, or brownish-purple, and may also be striped or spotted.

After the storm had passed...we hung our hammocks in a shelter, some little distance from the hut. I was scarcely protected from the weather by the one, frail wall; through the gaps in the roof shone the full moon as she moved across the clear sky...We left early after a hurried coffee, and made a very successful collection in the igapó. But I regretted the lack of a small canoe, for in the boat it was impossible to penetrate the forest and to follow the inviting channels through the igapó as the vegetation was too dense. But on the outskirts, growing low in the branches of a Macrolobium, I found my first Mormodes amazonica.
[M. Mee, **Flowers of the Amazon,** Plate 21]

Mormodes buccinator, Margaret Mee field sketch

Margaret Mee

Clowesia warczewitzii, 1971 (family Orchidaceae)
Pencil and gouache on paper. 661 x 483 mm.
Collection: Library, Royal Botanic Gardens, Kew.

The genus *Clowesia*, containing only five species, was named in honor of the British horticulturist Rev. John Clowes by John Lindley in the *Botanical Register* in 1843. Similar to *Catasetum*, it is distinguishable from that genus by its bisexual flowers and differing pollinating mechanism.

Clowesia warczewitzii, distributed from Costa Rica to coastal Ecuador and eastward to Colombia, Venezuela and Brazil, was named after the celebrated orchid collector Josef Warscewicz (1812-66). This epiphytic orchid produces pale green, frilled flowers with darker green lines, borne on pendent inflorescences.

The Araça has more terra firma than the Demini which is all igapó... The river narrowed considerably and we found the way blocked by a wall of rock. Huge stones confronted us over which the river cascaded in a raging torrent...I asked Tushaua Araken if he would take me into the forest before leaving, and he agreed willingly. We set off in his dugout canoe to thick forest lying behind a wall of rocks, over which roared the cascading falls. Araken maneuvered the canoe skillfully into calm waters, and we landed on a rocky shore where we found ourselves in the loveliest glade, green with ferns and mosses, sparkling with little streams trickling through crevices. Here I made a wonderful find: a small green-flowered orchid, Clowesia warczewitzii, was growing on a moss-covered branch. The species had not been seen by botanists for eighty years.

[M. Mee, (edited T. Morrison) **Margaret Mee: In Search of Flowers of the Amazon Forests,** Journey Six]

Clowesia warczewitzii Ltd.
Rio Araca, Rio alegre, Am.
April, 1971

Margaret Mee

Scuticaria steelii, 1972 (family Orchidaceae)
Pencil and gouache on paper. 661 x 483 mm.
Collection: Library, Royal Botanic Gardens, Kew.

Scuticaria, a small genus of only five species, was described in 1843 by the eminent botanist John Lindley, who based its name on the Latin *scutica* (whip), in reference to the long, whip-like leaves that may reach up to 1.5 meters in length.

Scuticaria steelii was named after Matthew Steele, who discovered this unusual orchid in Guyana in 1836. In the wild, it occurs in the Guianas, Venezuela, Colombia, and Brazil and produces fragrant, pale yellow flowers, blotched with reddish-brown and measuring five to seven cm in diameter. The plant in the painting was collected along the Rio Negro, where it was found growing on a Jará palm (*Leopoldinia pulchra*) in igapó forest.

We are now on the return journey and hoping that the petrol will last until Tapuracuara - there is one tin left and a little in the tank. So we are meandering with the current which is strong here, hoping to eke it out...It has been a fantastic trip and my finds have been very good, many beautiful orchids including the famed 'blue' Acacallis cyanea, the lovely perfumed Scuticaria steelii, yellow, spotted with chestnut, whose cylindrical leaves hang a metre long; very interesting bromeliads one of which I am certain is a new species, found growing in the darkest part of the igapó like a candelabrum, with small blue florets, as transparent as crystal.

[M. Mee, **Flowers of the Amazon,** Plate 20]

Scuticaria steelii, Margaret Mee field sketch

Scuticaria steelii Lindl.
Amazonas, Rio Negro
May, 1972

Margaret Mee

Galeandra devoniana, 1984 (family Orchidaceae)
Pencil and gouache on paper. 661 x 483 mm.
Collection: Library, Royal Botanic Gardens, Kew.

Exploring in South America on behalf of the Royal Geographical Society, Sir Robert Schomburgk first discovered *Galeandra devoniana* near Barcelos on the Rio Negro, and named it in honor of the Duke of Devonshire, an ardent collector of orchids. The genus *Galeandra*, containing 26 species, is distributed from Mexico to Bolivia, with the strongest occurrence in the Amazon region, where it grows on trees along waterways or on floodplains at elevations ranging from sea level to 500 meters.

Galeandra devoniana bears deciduous leaves and fragrant, long-lasting flowers, varying in color from brownish-green and veined with maroon stripes to deep purple-brown and edged with green. This tall, elegant plant was collected from the Lago Sapuacá in Oriximiná, Rio Trombetas, Pará.

...we entered a narrow parana bordered with Jara palms, small trees which, during high waters, are half or even completely submerged. On their fibrous stems clung Galeandra devoniana, an orchid with bell-shaped blooms of purple, brown and creamy white. Their perfume filled the air.

[M. Mee (edited T. Morrison), **Margaret Mee: In Search of Flowers of the Amazon Forests,** Journey Six]

Galeandra devoniana, Margaret Mee field sketch

Galeandra dives, 1985 (family Orchidaceae)
Pencil and gouache on paper. 661 x 483 mm.
Collection: Library, Royal Botanic Gardens, Kew.

Galeandra is a genus of approximately twenty-six species, distributed from Mexico to Bolivia but most strongly represented in the Amazon region. The species *Galeandra dives* is distributed in the Guianas, Venezuela, Colombia, and Brazil. This little known orchid is not known in cultivation, while in the wild it has been reported growing epiphytically on trees over river banks.

The flowers of this delicate orchid are golden brown with an unusual maroon tinge. The lip together with the spur measure around six cm. long. Margaret's painting was drawn from a plant collected from Lago Caipuru, Rio Trombetas, Pará.

... I had to rise early next day for a two-day walk in the Serra...We paddled upstream for about an hour with no rapids to hinder us, while I kept my gaze riveted on the banks where I was rewarded by finding the bromeliad, Aechmea chantinii, and a fine, sweetly- perfumed Galeandra orchid.

[M. Mee (edited T. Morrison), **Margaret Mee: In Search of Flowers of the Amazon Forests,** Journey Three]

Galeandra dives, Margaret Mee field sketch

Margaret Mee
June, 1985

Galeandra sp.
Lago Caipuru,
Jacunetas, Pará

Vriesea erythrodactylon, undated (family Bromeliaceae)
Pencil and gouache on paper. 661 x 483 mm.
Collection: National Museum of Natural History, Smithsonian Institution.

Directly translated, the name given to this species of *Vriesea* by the distinguished Belgian botanist Edouard Morren means Red-fingered Vriesea. The single spike is striking with its coloring of green edged in red, and its leaves are noteworthy by themselves, with their dark purple and brown sheaths. Although it is not common in cultivation, Professor Morren reportedly had it growing in his gardens in Belgium as early as 1882. Distributed on the eastern coast of Brazil, it is found from Espirito Santo to Santa Catarina, thriving along the coastal areas. Margaret collected her plant at Caraguatatuba, north of Santos.

Vriesea erythrodactylon, Margaret Mee field sketch

Vriesea erythrodactylon

Margaret Mee

Vriesea ensiformis var. bicolor, undated (family Bromeliaceae)
Pencil and gouache on paper. 661 x 483 mm.
Collection: National Museum of Natural History, Smithsonian Institution.

The species *Vriesea ensiformis,* discovered by the Franciscan monk Frei Vellozo around the year 1790, is commonly seen along the coastal rainforest, from Bahia to Santa Catarina. Its variety, however, was not discovered for yet another century and remains unknown outside its original state of São Paulo.

The 20 to 30 leaves of *Vriesea ensiformis* var. bicolor form the characteristic funnel-form rosette and the bicolorous character of its inflorescence is highly ornamental. Margaret's plant was collected from Paranapiacaba.

Vriesea ensiformis var. bicolor, Margaret Mee field sketch

Vriesea enseformis, var.
bicolor   Paranapiacaba
São Paulo   Margaret Mee

Margaret Mee

Aechmea fosteriana, undated (family Bromeliaceae)
Pencil and gouache on paper. 661 x 483 mm.
Collection: National Museum of Natural History, Smithsonian Institution.

The Brazilian species *Aechmea fosteriana* was collected by and named for the American bromeliad collector and explorer Mulford B. Foster, who co-founded the Bromeliad Society in 1950. Its beautifully variegated leaves and striking inflorescence, with dark red bracts, combine to make this bromeliad one of the most outstanding *Aechmea* plants. The plant in this painting came from the well-known gardens of Dr. Roberto Burle Marx, Brazil's most celebrated landscape architect.

Margaret Mee

Aechmea fraterniana
Burle Marx from Santa Teresa
Espirito Santo

Tillandsia linearis, undated (family Bromeliaceae)
Pencil and gouache on paper. 661 x 483 mm.
Collection: National Museum of Natural History, Smithsonian Institution.

The genus *Tillandsia*, established in 1753 by Linnaeus, was named in honor of the Finnish botanist Elias Tillands (1640-1693). With its more than 400 species, it has the distinction of being the largest genus in the Bromeliaceae family and, to many collectors, it is also the most interesting, since it comprises numerous smaller species conducive to being grown in terrariums or small greenhouses. The most commonly known species of this genus widely distributed in the United States, is *Tillandsia usneoides*, the famous "Spanish Moss".

Tillandsia linearis was discovered by the Franciscan monk Frei Vellozo, who labored for eight years, from 1782 through 1790, to prepare a flora of the plants of Rio de Janeiro, only to die several years prior to its publication. It has a somewhat restricted distribution, occurring in Goiás and southeastern Brazil, from the vicinity of Rio to Paraná. Margaret's plant comes from the lovely region of Parati in western Rio de Janeiro, reportedly very close to where Vellozo first discovered this species.

Tillandsia linearis, Margaret Mee field sketch

Margaret Mee

Tillandsia stricta
Florale, Rio

Margaret Mee

Vriesea guttata, undated (family Bromeliaceae)
Pencil and gouache on paper. 661 x 483 mm.
Collection: National Museum of Natural History, Smithsonian Institution.

The species *Vriesea guttata* was described in 1875 from plants grown from seeds that had been brought to Europe from Santa Catarina, Brazil in 1870. Its name is derived from the Latin gutta (spotted), in reference to its spotted leaves. Ten years later, in 1880, the distinguished Belgian botanist Edouard Morren featured this species in the publication, *La Belgique Horticole*, which had been started by his father.

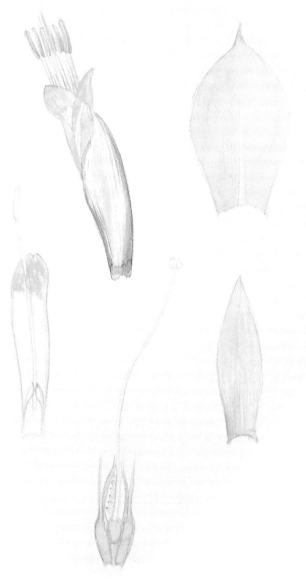

With a distribution restricted to Brazil, *V. guttata* is found in greatest concentration in Santa Catarina, the region where it was initially collected. It has also been found in various locations along the coastal rainforest, including the Organ Mountains north of Rio, where Margaret collected the plant depicted in this painting.

Vriesea guttata, Margaret Mee field sketch

Margaret Mee

Vriesea guttata
Serra dos Orgãos, Rio

Quesnelia arvensis, 1963 (family Bromeliaceae)
Pencil and gouache on paper. 661 x 483 mm.
Collection: National Museum of Natural History, Smithsonian Institution.

The genus *Quesnelia,* comprising approximately 12 species, was described in 1842 and named for a French consul, Quesnel. These plants, distributed exclusively in eastern Brazil, form a large rosette with rigid, gray-green leaves edged with spines. The inflorescence is borne on a single erect spike.

The accuracy and delicacy of Margaret Mee's draftsmanship is particularly noticeable in the detailed studies of the flower parts, shown at the bottom of the page.

Quesnelia arvensis, Margaret Mee field sketch

Margaret Mee

Tillandsia stricta, undated (family Bromeliaceae)
Pencil and gouache on paper. 661 x 483 mm.
Collection: National Museum of Natural History, Smithsonian Institution.

Tillandsia stricta is one of the most popular species of the genus as it flowers frequently with a colorful, cone-like inflorescence four to five cm. in length. It is distributed not only in Rio de Janeiro and its immediate vicinity, but has extended its occurrence north to Venezuela and south to Argentina, where it grows epiphytically on trees and shrubs. It is also commonly seen growing on telephone wires in more populated areas. Margaret Mee's plant, collected near São Paulo, is very similar in form to the original featured in the *Botanical Magazine* as early as 1813.

Tillandsia stricta
15 km Miracatu, B.12.2

Margaret Mee

Margaret Mee

Neoregalia concentrica, 1962 (family Bromeliaceae)
Pencil and gouache on paper. 661 x 483 mm.
Collection: São Paulo Botanical Institute.

The family *Bromeliaceae*, consisting of approximately 2000 species, is exclusively of the Americas, with the exception of *Pitcairnia feliciana*, which is found in West Africa. The Swedish naturalist Carl Linnaeus formally established the genus *Bromelia*, honoring Olaf Bromel, a distinguished 19th century Swedish botanist.

Neoregalia concentrica grows epiphytically on trees in the forest and is found in the Serra dos Orgaos, State of Rio de Janeiro. Its name refers to the arrangement of its violet flowers, clustered in concentric circles in the center of the rosette.

So we set out with a fresh wind blowing and the sun hidden by clouds, which was good for the many plants already filling the prow...But the river proved a marvelous one to explore, and I added many interesting plants to my collection. Among them...many bromeliads including aechmeas, billbergias, araeococcus, neoregelias, and guzmanias...
[M. Mee, (edited T. Morrison) **Margaret Mee: In Search of Flowers of the Amazon Forests,** Journey Eight]

Neoregelia sp.
Espírito Santo

Margaret Mee

Margaret Mee

Nidularium innocentii var. wittmackianum, 1961 (family Bromeliaceae)
Pencil and gouache on paper. 661 x 483 mm.
Collection: São Paulo Botanical Institute.

This species was named after the Marquis de St. Innocent, the French publisher and bromeliad enthusiast, with the variety name honoring Ludwig Wittmack, the German botanist. Margaret Mee painted this plant portrait during her early years in Brazil, when she was working closely with Dr. Lyman Smith to depict the bromeliads of eastern Brazil. A common epiphyte in tropical rainforests, it is distributed along the eastern coastal regions from São Paulo to Santa Catarina.

Nidulariums, like the Neoregelias, make superb indoor plants with their small to medium size, easy maintenance, and striking leaf color. They do, however, require more light than Neoregalias. There are thirty-five species in the genus *Nidularium*, all of which are located in eastern Brazil.

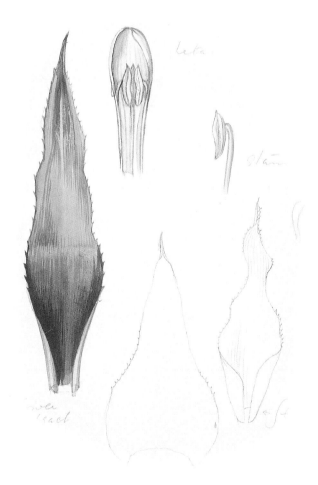

Nidularium innocentii var. wittmackianum, Margaret Mee field sketch

Nidularium innocentii
var.
Dezembro 1980
Reserva Florestal,
Caraguatatuba, S. Paulo

Margaret Mee

Margaret Mee

Nidularium antoineanum, 1961 (family Bromeliaceae)
Pencil and gouache on paper. 661 x 483 mm.
Collection: São Paulo Botanical Institute.

The genus *Nidularium* derives its name from the Latin *nidulus* (small nest), referring to the nest-like shape of the flower clusters. Like *Neoregalia* species, *Nidularium* form a water reservoir with their rosettes. It is distinguishable by virtue of its funnel-shaped tanks as opposed to the tubular shape of *Aechmea* and *Billbergia* genera. *Nidularium* are exclusive to Brazil.

The species is named in honor of the Austrian horticulturist Franz Antoine Jr., Director of the Schönbrunn Gardens, Vienna. This epiphytic plant is from Boracéia, Estado de São Paulo. Margaret Mee's painting succeeds in capturing the delicacy of this plant with its cluster of blue flowers surrounded by brilliant wine-colored bracts.

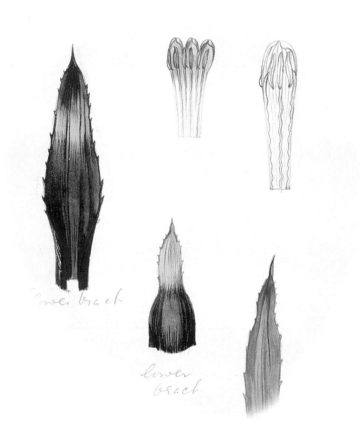

Nidularium antoineanum, Margaret Mee field sketch

Margaret Mee

Streptocalyx poeppigii, 1962 (family Bromeliaceae)
Pencil and gouache on paper. 661 x 483 mm.
Collection: São Paulo Botanical Institute.

Margaret Mee created two paintings of *Streptocalyx poeppigii,* completed at various points in her career as an artist. The earlier work, completed in 1962 and drawn from the Collections of the São Paulo Botanical Institute, is in the classic style with the plant placed against a stark white background. In her later painting, Margaret expressed her concern for the delicate balance of the Amazon ecosystem by setting the plant against a backdrop of rainforest trees and plants, depicting its natural habitat. The latter work, drawn from the Collections of the Royal Botanic Gardens, Kew, was completed in 1985, three years prior to her death.

The heat in Manaus was overwhelming...I was eager to start collecting and painting, so when Dr. Rodrigues of the Botanical Research Institution suggested a drive to the forest reserve named after the famous Brazilian botanist Adolfo Ducke, I enthusiastically agreed. Once inside, the temperature became bearable, for the thick canopy of the trees formed a barrier between us and the burning sun. In the less shady places a very beautiful passion-flower, full of dark blue blooms, trailed its long stems. The most magnificent spectacle was a group of bromeliads, Streptocalyx poeppigii growing on a fallen tree. There were three tall spikes of flowers which gleamed amethyst and pink in the beams of sunlight which slanted through the trees.

[M. Mee, **Flowers of the Brazilian Forest,** Plate 24]

Streptocalyx poeppigii, Margaret Mee field sketch

Aechmea poeppigii
Phot: Reserva Ducke.
Manaus, Amazonas, III.1984   Margaret Mee

Vriesea jonghei, 1961 (family Bromeliaceae)
Pencil and gouache on paper. 661 x 483 mm.
Collection: São Paulo Botanical Institute.

Vriesea jonghei was introduced to European gardens by the Belgian horticulturist M. de Jonghei. Distributed in Central and South American forests, this stunning plant occurs most frequently in Brazil's southern coastal mountains, or the Serra do Mar. *V. jonghei* is valued for its striking inflorescence, with large yellow flowers and mustard-brown floral bracts, densely speckled with brown spots.

Vriesea jonghei, Margaret Mee field sketch

Margaret Mee (signature)

Paintings by Margaret Mee Scholars

Clitoria fairchildiana, 1994 (family Leguminosae)
Pencil and watercolour on paper. 541x384 mm.
Collection: Private collector; Rio de Janeiro, Brazil
Artist: Malena Barretto, 1990 Margaret Mee Scholar

Named for David Fairchild, founder of the Fairchild Tropical Garden in Miami, Florida, *Clitoria fairchildiana* develops as a tree that may exceed eight meters in height. The petals of its delicately scented flowers are violet with red purple markings that turn pink to pink-purple when dried. This tropical species was introduced into cultivation by seed derived from Amazonia.

Desmoncus sp., 1993 (family Palmae)
Pencil and watercolour on paper. 541x 384 mm.
Collection: Private Collector; Rio de janeiro, Brazil
Artist: Dulce Nascimento, 1991 Margaret Mee Scholar

Most species of *Desmoncus* are slender, spiny palms of the lowlands, often found in such open areas as swamps and riverbanks and occasionally in the undergrowth of tropical rainforest. Distributed from Mexico southward to Brazil and Bolivia, many *Desmoncus* species provide cane for a variety of native products such as cordage, basket frames and low-cost furniture. Although the genus *Desmoncus* represents the New World equivalent of the Asiatic rattans, its species are not utilized locally to the same degree.

Desmoncus sp.
"Jacitara"
Ilha Combu, munic. Acará, Pará.
segmento do ramo, cacho de frutos, folha e ápice foliar

Jula Nascimento
abril, 1993.

Couepia longipendula, 1994 (family Chrysobalanaceae)
Pencil and watercolour on paper. 541x384 mm.
Collection: Private collector; Sao Paulo, Brazil
Artist: Hiroe Sasaki, 1992 Margaret Mee Scholar

Originating in the Amazonian rainforest, this species grows as a tree 5 to 30 meters tall, with a much spreading crown that cascades down to almost ground level. It is remarkable for the length of its striking flower stalks which may reach 60 cm in length. The plant depicted in this painting was collected in the area of Manaus, where the species is cultivated for its edible cotyledons.

SELECT BIBLIOGRAPHY

Allen, O.N. and Ethel K. Allen. The Leguminosae. Madison: University of Wisconsin Press, 1981.

Barth, Friedrich G. Insects and Flowers: The Biology of a Partnership. (Translated by M.A. Biederman-Thorson). Princeton: Princeton University Press, 1985.

Bates, Henry Walter. The Naturalist on the River Amazons. London: John Murray, 1892.

Bechtel, H., P. Cribb and E. Launert. The Manual of Cultivated Orchid Species. Poole: Blandford Press, 1981.

Beddall, Barbara G. (ed.). Wallace and Bates in the Tropics. An Introduction to the History of Natural Selection. London: The Macmillan Co., 1969.

Benzing, David H. The Biology of the Bromeliads. Eureka: Mad River Press Inc., 1980.

Berry, Fred and W. John Kress. Heliconia. Washington D.C.: Smithsonian Institution Press, 1991.

Blunt, Wilfred and William T. Stearn. The Art of Botanical Illustration. London: Collins, 1950.

Blunt, Wilfred and William T. Stearn. The Art of Botanical Illustration (2nd Edn.). London: Collins, 1994.

Bown, D. Aroids: Plants of the Arum Family. London: Century Hutchinson, 1988.

Burbidge, Dr. Brinsley. "Botanical Theatre." The Illustrated London News, London. Autumn, 1989.

Calder, Malcolm and Peter Bernhardt (ed.). The Biology of Mistletoes. Sydney: Academic Press, 1983.

Calmann, Gerta. Ehret: Flower Painter Extraordinary. Boston: New York Graphic Society. 1977.

Cowan, R.S. "A Taxonomic Revision of the Genus Heterostemon (Leguminosae-Caesalpinioideae)." Proceedings of the Koninklijke Nederlandse Akademie van Wetenschappen, 79, series C. (1976): 43-53.

Cowell, Adrian. The Decade of Destruction: The Crusade to Save the Amazon Rain Forest. New York: Henry Holt and Co., 1990.

Cribb, Phillip. The Forgotten Orchids of Alexandré Brun. New York: Grove Press, 1992.

Cullen, J. The Orchid Book. Cambridge: Cambridge University Press, 1992.

Cunningham, Sue and Ghillean T. Prance. Out of the Amazon. London: Her Majesty's Stationery Office, 1992.

Dean, W. Brazil and the Struggle of Rubber: A Study in Environmental History. London: Cambridge University Press, 1987.

Desmond, R. Dictionary of British and Irish Botanists and Horticulturists. London: Taylor and Francis, 1977; and Rev. ed., 1994.

Desmond, Ray. Kew: The History of the Royal Botanic Gardens. London: Harvill Press and Royal Botanic Gardens, Kew, 1995.

Dickenson, John. "Bates, Wallace and Economic Botany in Mid-Nineteenth Century Amazonia." Richard Spruce (1817-1893). Botanist and Explorer, 6. (1996): 65-80.

Dressler, Robert L. The Orchids: Natural History and Classification. Cambridge: Harvard University Press, 1981.

Drew, William B. "Cinchona Work in Ecuador by Richard Spruce and by United States Botanists in the 1940s." Richard Spruce (1817-1893), Botanist and Explorer, (1996) 12. (1996): 157-161.

Elliott, Brent. Treasures of the Royal Horticultural Society. London: Herbert Press, Ltd., 1994.

Evans, Anne-Marie and Donn Evans. An Approach to Botanical Painting in Watercolour, Rutland: Hannaford and Evans, 1993.

Ewan, Joseph. "Tracking Richard Spruce's Legacy from George Bentham to Edward Whymper." Richard Spruce (1817-1893), Botanist and Explorer, 4. (1996): 41-49.

Field, David V. "Richard Spruce's Economic Botany Collections at Kew." Richard Spruce (1817-1893), Botanist and Explorer, 21. (1996): 245-264.

Foshay, Ella M. Reflections of Nature, Flowers in American Art. New York: Alfred A. Knopf, in association with the Whitney Museum of American Art, 1984.

Fundaçao Botânica Margaret Mee (ed.). Margaret Mee: Life and Legacy. Rio de Janiero: Museum of Modern Art, 1992.

Furneaux, Robin. The Amazon, The Story of a Great River. New York: Hamish Hamilton, 1969.

Gentry, Alwin H. "Studies in Bignoniaceae 19: Generic Mergers and New Species of South American Bignoniaceae." Annals of the Missouri Botanical Garden. (ed. G. Davidse, W.G. D'Arcy, J.D. Dwyer and P. Goldblatt). 63 no.1. (1976): 54-58.

Gentry, Alwyn H. "Bignoniaceae." Annals of the Missouri Botanical Garden, 60 no.3. (1973): 781-978.

Goulding, Michael Amazon: The Flooded Forest. New York: Sterling Publishing Co., 1990.

Gradwohl, Judith and Russell Greenberg. Saving the Tropical Forests. Washington D.C.: Island Press, 1988.

Hemming, John. Amazon Frontier: the Defeat of the Brazilian Indians. Cambridge: Harvard University Press, 1987.

Hemming, John. Red Gold. The Conquest of the Brazilian Indians. London: Macmillan, 1978.

Hepper, F. Nigel (ed.). Plant Hunting for Kew. London: Her Majesty's Stationery Office, 1989.

Holmgren, Noel H. and Bobbi Angell. Botanical Illustration: Preparation for Publication. New York: New York Botanical Garden, 1986.

Hulton, Paul and Lawrence Smith. Flowers in Art from East and West. London: British Museum Publications, 1979.

Isley, Paul T. III, Tillandsia. Gardena: Botanical Press, 1987.

Kaden, Vera. The Illustration of Plants and Gardens 1500-1850. London: V&A Museum, 1983.

Kramer, Jack. Bromeliads. New York: Harper and Row, 1981.

Leme, Elton M.C. and Luiz Claudio Marigo. Bromeliads in the Brazilian Wilderness. Rio de Janeiro: Marigo Comunicacao Visual, 1993.

Linden, Jean. Lindenia: Iconographie des Orchidees. Gand: Compagnie Continentale D'Horticuture, 1886.

Mabberley, D.J. The Plant Book. Cambridge: Cambridge University Press, 1987.

Masters, Charles O. Encyclopedia of the Water-Lily. Neptune City: T.F.H. Publications, Inc. Ltd., 1974.

Mayo, Simon. Margaret Mee's Amazon. London: Royal Botanic Gardens, Kew, 1988.

McQueen, Jim and Barbara McQueen. Orchids of Brazil. Portland: Timber Press, 1993.

Mee, Margaret. Flowers of the Amazon. Rio de Janiero: Distribuidora Record, 1980.

Mee, Margaret. Flowers of the Brazilian Forests. London: The Tryon Gallery, 1968.

Mee, Margaret. Margaret Mee: In Search of Flowers of the Amazon Forests. (ed. Tony Morrison). Woodbridge: Nonesuch Expeditions, 1988.

Miller, David, Richard Warren and Izabel Moura Miller. Orchids of the High Mountain Atlantic Rain Forest in Southeastern Brazil. Rio de Janeiro: Salamandra Consultoria Editorial, 1994.

Pabst, G.F.J. and F. Dungs. Orchidaceae Brasilienses, 2 vols. Hildesheim: Brucke-Verlag, Kurt Schmersow, 1975-1977.

Perry, Frances. The Water Garden. New York: Van Nostrand Reinhold Co., 1981.

Perry, Frances. Water Gardening. London: Country Life, Ltd., 1961.

Porter, Duncan M. "With Humboldt, Wallace and Spruce at San Carlos de Rio Negro." Richard Spruce (1817-1893), Botanist and Explorer, 5. (1996): 51-63.

Prance, Ghillean T. and Thomas S. Elias. Extinction is Forever. New York: New York Botanical Garden, 1977.

Prance, G.T. and T.E. Lovejoy. Amazonia (Key Environments Series). Oxford: Pergamon Press and IUCN, 1985.

Prance, G.T. and S.A. Mori. Flora Neotropica, Monograph 21 (1-2). New York: New York Botanical Garden, 1979.

Pridgeon, Alex (ed.). The Illustrated Encyclopedia of Orchids. Portland: Timber Press, 1992.

Rauh, Werner. The Bromeliad Lexicon. (ed. Peter Temple). (Translated by Peter Temple and Harvey L. Kendall). London: Blandford, 1990.

Rix, Martyn. The Art of the Plant World: The Great Botanical Illustrators and their Work. New York: The Overlook Press, 1981.

Romero, Gustavo A. "Orchidaceae Spruceanae. Orchids Collected by Spruce in South America." Richard Spruce (1817-1893), Botanist and Explorer, 14. (1996): 171-182.

Rosenbaum S. P. (ed.). The Bloomsbury Group. Toronto: University of Toronto Press, 1995.

Sandeman, C. "Richard Spruce: Portrait of a Great Englishman." Journal of the Royal Horticultural Society (1949): 74.

Schultes, R.E. "Richard Spruce Still Lives." Northern Gardener, 7. (1953): 20-27, 55-61, 87-93, 121-125. [Also issued as repaginated reprint, pp. 1-27.]

Schultes, R.E. "Margaret Mee and Richard Spruce." Naturalist, 115. (1990): 146-148.

Schultes, Richard Evans. "Richard Spruce, the Man." Richard Spruce (1817-1893). Botanist and Explorer, 1. (1996): 15-25.

Scrase, David. Flowers of Three Centuries, One Hundred Drawings and Watercolours from the Broughton Collection, organized and circulated by the International Exhibitions Foundation, Washington, D.C., 1983.

Sheehan, Tom and Marion Sheehan. An Illustrated Survey of Orchid Genera. Portland: Timber Press, 1994.

Sherwood, Shirley. Contemporary Botanical Artists. London: Weidenfeld and Nicolson in Association with the Royal Botanic Gardens, Kew, 1996.

Silcock, Lisa (ed.). The Rainforests: A Celebration. San Francisco: Chronicle Books, 1989.

Smith, Anthony. Explorers of the Amazon. London: Viking, 1990.

Smith, L.B. "Notes on Bromeliaceae". Phytologia, 13. (March 1996): 84-161.

Smith, L.B. and R.J. Downs. Flora Neotropica, Monograph 14 (1-3). New York: New York Botanical Gardens, 1974-1979.

Smith, Lyman B. and Margaret Mee. The Bromeliads. S. Brunswick: A.S. Barnes and Co., 1969.

Smith, N.J.H. "Relevance of Spruce's Work to Conservation and Management of Natural Resources in Amazonia." Richard Spruce (1817-1893), Botanist and Explorer, 19. (1996): 227-237.

Spruce, Richard. Notes of a Botanist on the Amazon and Andes. (ed. Alfred Russel Wallace). London: Macmillan and Co. Ltd., 1908.

Stearn, William T. Botanical Latin, 4th edn. Brunel House: David and Charles, 1992.

Stearn, William T. Flower Artists of Kew, London: Herbert Press in association with the Royal Botanic Gardens, Kew, 1990.

Stephenson, C.M. Looking at Flowers. West Palm Beach: K.P. International Inc., 1994.

Stewart, Joyce and William T. Stearn. The Orchid Paintings of Franz Bauer. London: Herbert Press in association with the Natural History Museum, 1993.

Stiff, Ruth L. A. Flowers from the Royal Gardens of Kew. Hanover: University Press of New England, 1988.

Stiff, Ruth L. A. "Richard Spruce and Margaret Mee: Explorers on the Rio Negro, a Century Apart." Richard Spruce (1817-1893), Botanist and Explorer, 7. (1996): 81-91.

Thornton, Robert. The Temple of Flora. Boston: New York Graphic Society, 1981.

Von Hagen, Victor Wolfgang. South America Called Them: Explorations of the Great Naturalists. New York: Alfred A. Knopf, 1945.

Wallace, Alfred Russel. A Narrative of Travels on the Amazon and Rio Negro, with an Account of the Native Tribes and Observations on the Climate, Geology and Natural History of the Amazon Valley. London: Reeve and Co., 1853.

Wanderley, Maria das Gracas Lapa (ed.). Bromélias Brasileiras: Aquarelas de Margaret Mee. São Paulo: Instituto de Botânica de São Paulo, 1992.

PAST EXHIBITIONS *

1958	Biblioteca Nacional do Rio de Janeiro, Brazil
	Instituto de Botânica de São Paulo, Brazil
1960	Royal Horticultural Society, London, England
1967	Museu de Arte de São Paulo, Brazil
	Dumbarton Oaks, Washington, D.C., USA
1968	Tryon Gallery, London, England
	Hunt Institute for Botanical Documentation, Pittsburgh, USA
1970	Tryon Gallery, London, England
1973	Moorland Gallery, London, England
1977	Moorland Gallery, London, England
1980	The British Museum (Natural History), London, England
1981	Museu Naval, Rio de Janeiro, Brazil
1982	Museu de Arte de São Paulo, Brazil
1983	Jardim Botânico, Rio de Janeiro, Brazil
1986	Missouri Botanical Garden, St. Louis, USA
1988	Kew Gardens Gallery, RBG, Kew, England
1990	Harewood House, Yorkshire, England
	Banco do Brazil, Rio de Janeiro, Brazil
1991	Palaçio Itamaraty, Brazilia, Brazil
	Hunterian Art Gallery, University of Glasgow, Scotland
1992	Museu do Arte Moderna, Rio de Janeiro, Brazil
	Museu de Arte de São Paulo, Brazil
1993	Liverpool Museum
	City Museum and Art Gallery, Bristol, England
1995	Camden Arts Centre, London, England
1996	Bodleian Library, Oxford, England

* Representing the paintings, field sketchbooks and notebooks of Margaret Mee,
drawn from various collections, both private and public.

INDEX OF PLATES